.

Facing History and Ourselves is an international educational and professional development organization whose mission is to use lessons of history to challenge teachers and their students to stand up to bigotry and hate. For more information about Facing History and Ourselves, please visit our website at www.facinghistory.org.

ISBN-13: 978-1-940457-39-0

ACKNOWLEDGMENTS

We would like to thank the following individuals and organizations for making possible the creation of this curriculum and professional development for Chicago Public Schools*:

Anonymous (2)

Aon Foundation

The Baskin Family Foundation

Christopher Family Foundation

The Crown Family

Karen Harrison and Walter Freedman

Jackson

Robert R. McCormick Foundation

Linda and Judd Miner

Oppenheimer Family Foundation

PPM America

Pritzker Pucker Family Foundation

The Segal Family Foundation

The Charles & M.R. Shapiro Foundation

Jill Garling and Tom Wilson

Zell Family Foundation

*Recognizing commitments made as of August 2021.

CONTENTS

PART 4: RADICAL RECONSTRUCTION AND INTERRACIAL DEMOCRACY

PART 5: BACKLASH AND THE FRAGILITY OF DEMOCRACY

PART 6: MEMORY AND LEGACY

SHARING OUR LEARNING: WRITING CONNECTIONS

LETTER TO STUDENT

Dear student,

Welcome. You are about to begin a unit of study created by our organization, Facing History & Ourselves. Facing History's mission is to use lessons of history to challenge teachers and their students (you!) to stand up to bigotry and hate. While you study this history, you will be exploring questions about yourself and your responsibility to others in the world around you. That is what we mean by "facing history and ourselves."

A former Facing History student explained, "When I took the Facing History course back in eighth grade, it helped me understand that history was a part of me and that I was a part of history. If I understood why people made the choices they did, I could better understand how I make choices and hopefully make the right ones."

This unit may be different from others you have experienced. It will ask you to explore questions such as: Who am I? What shapes who I am becoming? Why do people form groups? What does it mean to belong? What happens when people are excluded? And it will ask you to consider these questions through the lens of history, exploring the decisions people made in the past, and the impact they have had on our world today. Although one person's choices may not seem important at the time, little by little, they define who we are as individuals, communities, and ultimately, as a nation.

This unit will ask you to use both your head and your heart to make sense of the choices people made in the past and the choices they continue to make today. You will be asked to listen carefully to the voices of others and may engage in discussions and with content that spark powerful emotions. It's important to process what you learn and take care of yourself through activities such as journaling and engaging in discussions with your classmates, teachers, and caregivers. By working together and supporting one another, we create a classroom where everyone can do their best learning.

We wish you a meaningful journey during which you engage in learning about the past and the present, about yourself, and about others.

Facing History & Ourselves

WHAT IS FACING HISTORY & OURSELVES?

Facing History & Ourselves is an international educational and professional development organization whose mission is to use lessons of history to challenge teachers and their students to stand up to bigotry and hate. For more information about Facing History & Ourselves, please visit our website at www.facinghistory.org.

WHAT IS THE FACING HISTORY SCOPE AND SEQUENCE?

While every Facing History class is unique, each is organized to follow our scope and sequence, which we often call the Facing History journey. The journey begins by examining common human behaviors, beliefs, and attitudes you can readily observe in your own life. Then, we explore a historical case study and analyze how those patterns of human behavior may have influenced the choices individuals made in the past—to participate, stand by, or stand up—in the face of injustice. Finally, we examine how the history you studied continues to influence our world today, and consider how you might choose to participate in bringing about a more humane, just, and compassionate world.

WHAT WILL YOU LEARN IN THIS UNIT?

Part 1: The Individual and Society introduces the concepts central to the unit—freedom, power, prejudice, and racism—by exploring the relationship between the individual and society. You will consider one of the most basic forms of connection between the individual and society, which had particular resonance for newly freed individuals during Reconstruction: names.

Part 2: We and They explores the socially constructed meaning of race and how that concept has been used historically to justify "in" groups and "out" groups in society. Diving into the history of Reconstruction, you will begin to reflect on the meaning of freedom and the question of whether or not one who is excluded from full and equal membership in society is truly free.

Part 3: Healing and Justice after War establishes the Civil War's upheaval as the backdrop to the challenges and conflicts of Reconstruction. You will analyze President Andrew Johnson's efforts to resolve these dilemmas, and, in the process, reflect on deeper issues of healing and justice in the aftermath of a profound transformation of society.

Part 4: Radical Reconstruction and Interracial Democracy examines the laws and amendments that were signal achievements of the Reconstruction era. In these lessons, you will explore the consequences of the laws passed as part of Radical Reconstruction, reflecting on how the revolutionary changes they set in motion in the late 1860s and early 1870s affected the strength of American democracy.

Part 5: Backlash and the Fragility of Democracy traces how an unprecedented period of interracial democracy triggered violent backlash in the South. These lessons will ask you to probe the effects of violence on a democracy while revisiting questions about the meaning of freedom and considering the limited choices available to African Americans as their rights were significantly curtailed.

Part 6: Memory and Legacy explores the way that the history of Reconstruction is remembered and the impact of its various legacies in contemporary society. The culminating activity for the unit is an "informed action" that will ask you to research and write a proposal for a public forum educating the community about one issue that was central during Reconstruction and remains unresolved today.

HOW SHOULD YOU PREPARE FOR THE UNIT?

Contracting

Throughout this unit, you will engage in discussions that may spark powerful emotions, and you will examine sources that depict racism and violence. When you create a class contract at the beginning of the unit, your teacher will ask you about what you'll need to have these discussions. Consider what helps you learn and take care of yourself. What might you add to the contract about what you need from your teacher and classmates? For example, you may want to include that you can choose to reflect privately in a journal instead of with a partner.

Checking in with Your People

We also invite you to check in regularly with trusted people in your life about your learning. You can use the following questions as a starting point for these conversations:

- How are you feeling about what you learned today?

- Was there a discussion, primary source reading, or a moment in class today that stood out to you? Why do you think it caught your attention?

- Is there anything you learned today that you find surprising? Or troubling? Why?

- What questions do you have about what you are learning that you might want to explore more?

Note about Violence and Dehumanizing Language in Primary Sources

This unit uses primary sources (sources that were created during the historical time period you will study) that include descriptions of violence, as well as racist and dehumanizing language and images. Each of the sources that has the n-word written out, as it originally appeared, has a note at the top. Before you read a source with racist or dehumanizing language, your teacher will remind you about the impact that this language can have and that it will not be read aloud. Remember that you can talk to your teacher, or other people in your life that you trust, about what you are thinking and feeling as you read and process these sources. Talk to your teacher about your classroom contract and opportunities for journaling and remember to check in with your people about what you are thinking and feeling.

HOW WILL YOU SHARE WHAT YOU LEARN?

Assessment: At the end of the unit, you will complete a summative performance task that has two parts: a writing prompt and an informed action. For the writing prompt, in an essay, you will construct an argument that addresses the essential question using specific claims and relevant evidence from historical and contemporary sources while acknowledging competing views.

In the performance task, you will apply lessons gained from your study of Reconstruction toward understanding contemporary challenges to freedom and equality. The informed action has three parts:

1. **UNDERSTAND:** You will pick a topic of debate that was central to the struggle for freedom and equality during Reconstruction and continues to be debated today. Examples of issues that were important during Reconstruction include but are not limited to:

   - Education
   - Political participation and citizenship (voting and office holding)
   - Economic equality
   - Equal protection of the law
   - The criminal justice system

2. **ASSESS:** In groups of three to five, you will conduct research to learn more about how your chosen topic is being discussed and debated today. *What are some of the important positions and perspectives on the topic? Who are key experts and stakeholders? What echoes of the Reconstruction era do you recognize in the debate today (both in the challenges faced and the solutions people are proposing to address the challenges)?*

3. **ACT:** In the same group, you will create a plan for organizing a public forum to educate a community (classroom, school, or neighborhood) about your chosen topic. Your group's plan should address the following questions:

   - *Whom will you invite to speak, and whom will you invite to be in the audience? Be sure to identify the local experts on the topic, who is directly impacted, and who might be capable of effecting change.*

   - *You may also want to consider whether you'll invite speakers with opposing viewpoints. If not, how will you offer the audience an opportunity to consider multiple perspectives?*

   - *What will be the venue and location for the forum? How will the location help you reach your intended audience?*

   - *What questions will you ask the speakers? How will your questions address the most important aspects of the debate?*

   - *How will you structure the agenda for the forum? How much time will you give for community members to weigh in? How much time for speakers?*

WRITING PROMPT

DIRECTIONS:
- Circle words you do not know or understand in the context of the prompt.
- Star words that seem to be the central ideas of the prompt.
- Underline all of the verbs that represent what you, as the writer, are supposed to do.
- Cross out any information that does not seem specifically relevant to the writing task.

What was the promise of Emancipation? To what extent was it fulfilled by Reconstruction?

In an essay, construct an argument that addresses this question using specific claims and relevant evidence from historical and contemporary sources while acknowledging competing views.

TWO NAMES, TWO WORLDS

In the poem below, Jonathan Rodríguez reflects on his name. How does his name "place him in the world"? How is it a mask, shield, or container?

Hi I'm Jon...........No — Jonathan

Wait — Jonathan *Rodríguez*

Hold on — Jonathan Rodríguez

My Name, Two names, two worlds

The duality of my identity like two sides of the same coin

With two worlds, there should be plenty of room

But where do I fit?

Where can I sit?

Is this seat taken? Or is that seat taken?

There never is quite enough room is there?

Two names, Two worlds

Where do I come from?

Born in the Washington heights of New York City

But raised in good ol' Connecticut

The smell of freshly mowed grass, autumn leaves

a traditional Latin American stew — *Sancocho*, Rice and Beans

The sound from Billy Joel's Piano Keys

a Dominican singer-songwriter — And the rhythm from *Juan Luis Guerra*

I'm from the struggle for broken dreams

of false promises

of houses with white picket fences

And 2.5 kids

fields of the Dominican Republic — The mountains and *campos de la Republica Dominicana*

And the mango trees

I'm not the typical kid from suburbia

Nor am I a smooth Latin cat

My head's in the clouds, my nose in a comic book

I get lost in the stories and art

I'm kinda awkward — so talkin' to the ladies is hard

a Dominican merengue singer; — I listen to *Fernando Villalona* and *Aventura* every chance I get,
a bachata music group

But don't make me dance *Merengue, Bachata*

styles of dance — or *Salsa*— I don't know the steps

I've learned throughout these past years

I am a mix of cultures, a mix of races

a race that is Black, white, and Taino — *"Una Raz encendida,*

Negra, Blanca y Taina"

a song — You can find me in the parts of a song, *en una cancion*

percussion instrument used in — You can feel my African Roots *en la Tambora*
merengue; percussion instrument
used in the Dominican Republic

My *Taino* screams *en la guira*

And the melodies of the lyrics are a reminder of my beautiful Spanish heritage

I am African, Taino and Spanish

A Fanboy, an athlete, a nerd, a student, an introvert

I am Dominican — I'm proud to say: *Yo soy Dominicano*

I'm proud to say, I am me

I am beginning to appreciate that I am

a beautiful blend — *Una bella mezcla*

I am beginning to see that this world is also a beautiful mix

of people, ideas and stories.

Is this seat taken?

Or is that seat taken?

Join me and take a seat,

Here we'll write our own stories[1]

---

[1] Jonathan Rodríguez, untitled poem.

NAMES AND FREEDOM

Historian Douglas Egerton explains one of the first tasks freedpeople had to complete once they were emancipated from slavery:

> Former slaves had to undertake a task unknown to free-born Americans. They had to adopt a surname. Although slaves often adopted family names for use among themselves, few masters wished to bestow upon their chattel the sense of dignity a surname implied.[1]

Historian Leon Litwack describes some of the factors freedpeople considered when adopting names:

> In some instances, Federal officials expedited the naming process by furnishing the names themselves, and invariably the name would be the same as that of the freedman's most recent master. But these appear to have been exceptional cases; the ex-slaves themselves usually took the initiative—like the Virginia mother who changed the name of her son from Jeff Davis, which was how the master had known him, to Thomas Grant, which seemed to suggest the freedom she was now exercising. Whatever names the freed slaves adopted, whether that of a previous master, a national leader, an occupational skill, a place of residence, or a color, they were most often making that decision themselves. That was what mattered.[2]

---

[1] Douglas R. Egerton, *The Wars of Reconstruction: The Brief, Violent History of America's Most Progressive Era* (New York: Bloomsbury Press, 2014), 40.

[2] Leon F. Litwack, *Been in the Storm So Long: The Aftermath of Slavery* (New York: Vintage Books, 1980), 251.

CHANGING NAMES

In the 1930s, ex-slave Martin Jackson explained why he chose his last name after Emancipation:

> The master's name was usually adopted by a slave after he was set free. This was done more because it was the logical thing to do and the easiest way to be identified than it was through affection for the master. Also, the government seemed to be in a almighty hurry to have us get names. We had to register as someone, so we could be citizens. Well, I got to thinking about all us slaves that was going to take the name Fitzpatrick. I made up my mind I'd find me a different one. One of my grandfathers in Africa was called Jeaceo, and so I decided to be Jackson.[1]

Dick Lewis Barnett and Phillip Fry were African American veterans of the Union Army during the Civil War. In 1911, Barnett and Fry's widow, Mollie, both applied for pensions from the government. This financial assistance was available to all Civil War veterans and their families. However, many African Americans faced a problem when they applied for their pensions. After the war ended and slavery was abolished, they exercised their freedom by changing their names. This meant that army records documented their service with their old names instead of their new ones. In order to receive their pensions decades later, these former soldiers and their family members had to demonstrate to the government that they were who they claimed to be. The following documents are excerpts from government records in which Dick Barnett and Mollie (Smith) Russell explain when and why they changed their names.

Testimony of Dick Lewis Barnett, May 17, 1911:

> I am 65 years of age; my post office address is Okmulgee Okla. I am a farmer.

> My full name is Dick Lewis Barnett. I am the applicant for pension on account of having served in Co. B. 77th U.S. Col Inf and Co. D. U.S. Col H Art under the name Lewis Smith which was the name I wore before the days of slavery were over. I am the identical person who served in the said companies under the name of Lewis Smith. I am the identical person who was named called and known as Dick Lewis Smith before the Civil War and during the Civil War and until I returned home after my military service . . .

> I was born in Montgomery County, Ala. the child of Phillis Houston, slave of Sol Smith. When I was born my mother was known as Phillis Smith and I took the name of Smith too. I was called mostly Lewis Smith till after the war, although I was named Dick Lewis Smith—Dick was the brother of John Barnett whom I learned was my father . . .

> When I got home after the war, I was wearing the name of Lewis Smith, but I found that the negroes after freedom, were taking the names of their father like the white folks. So I asked my mother and she told me my father [was] John Barnett, a white man, and I took up the name of Barnett . . .

Testimony of Mollie Russell (widow of Phillip Fry), September 19, 1911:

Q. Tell me the name you were called before you met Phillip Fry?

A. Lottie Smith was my name and what they called me before I met Phillip and was married to him.

Q. Who called you by that name and where was it done?

A. I was first called by that name in the family of Col. Morrow in whose service I was in Louisville, Ky., just after the war. I worked for him as nurse for his children, and my full and correct name was OCTAVIA, but the family could not "catch on" to that long name and called me "LOTTIE" for short. LOTTIE had been the name of the nurse before me and so they just continued that same name. I was called by that name all the time I was with the Morrows. . . .

Q. Besides the Morrows, whom else did you live with in Louisville?

A. Mr. Thomas Jefferson of Louisville, bought me when I was three years of age from Mr. Dearing. I belonged to him until emancipation. They called me "OCK". They cut it off from OCTAVIA. It was after emancipation on that I went back to work for Col. Morrow and where I got the name "Lottie," as already explained. I liked the name better than Octavia, and so I took it with me to Danville, and was never called anything else there than that name. . . .

Q. How did you ever come by the name of "Mollie"?

A. After I had returned to Louisville from Danville, My sister, Lizzie White, got to calling me Mollie, and it was with her that the name started.

Q. Where did you get the maiden name of Smith from?

A. My mother's name was Octavia Smith and it was from her that I got it but where the name came from to her I never knew. I was only three years old when she died. No, I don't know to whom she belonged before she was brought from Virginia to Kentucky.[2]

[1] Norman R. Yetman, ed., *Voices from Slavery: 100 Authentic Slave Narratives* (Dover Publications, 2012), 175.

[2] Civil War Pension File of Lewis Smith (alias Dick Lewis Barnett), Co. B, 77th US Colored Infantry, and Co. D, 10th US Colored Heavy Artillery, Record Group 15, Records of the Department of Veterans Affairs, National Archives, Washington, DC.

WHICH ONE OF THESE THINGS IS NOT LIKE THE OTHERS?

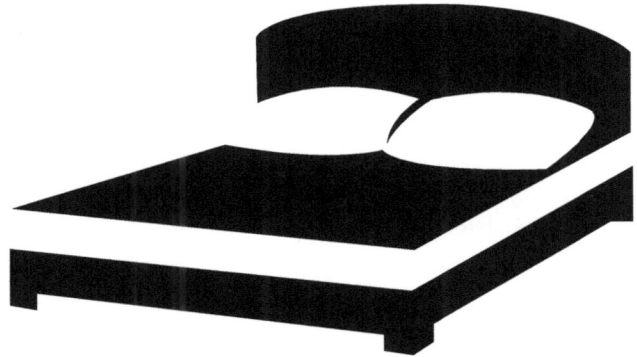

MAKING ALL THE DIFFERENCE

Legal scholar Martha Minow writes about the consequences of the way we respond to differences between us:

> When we identify one thing as unlike the others, we are dividing the world; we use our language to exclude, to distinguish—to discriminate. . . . Of course, there are "real differences" in the world; each person differs in countless ways from each other person. But when we simplify and sort, we focus on some traits rather than others, and we assign consequences to the presence and absence of the traits we make significant. We ask, "What's the new baby?"—and we expect as an answer, boy or girl. That answer, for most of history, has spelled consequences for the roles and opportunities available to that individual. And when we respond to persons' traits rather than their conduct, we may treat a given trait as a justification for excluding someone we think is "different." We feel no need for further justification: we attribute the consequences to the differences we see. We neglect other traits that may be shared. And we neglect how each of us, too, may be "different."[1]

[1] Martha Minow, *Making All the Difference* (Ithaca, NY: Cornell University Press, 1990), 3–4.

CIRCLES OF RESPONSIBILITY / UNIVERSE OF OBLIGATION

• In Circle 1, write your name.

• In Circle 2, write the name of people to whom you feel the greatest obligation—for example, people for whom you'd be willing to take a great risk or put yourself in peril (you don't have to write actual names; you could refer to a group of people, such as "my family").

• In Circle 3, write the names of the people on the next level—that is, people to whom you feel some responsibility, but not as great as for those in circle 2.

• In Circle 4, write the names of the people on the next level—people to whom you feel some responsibility, but not as great as for those in circle 3.

• To whom do you feel no sense of responsibility? List these groups outside circle 4.

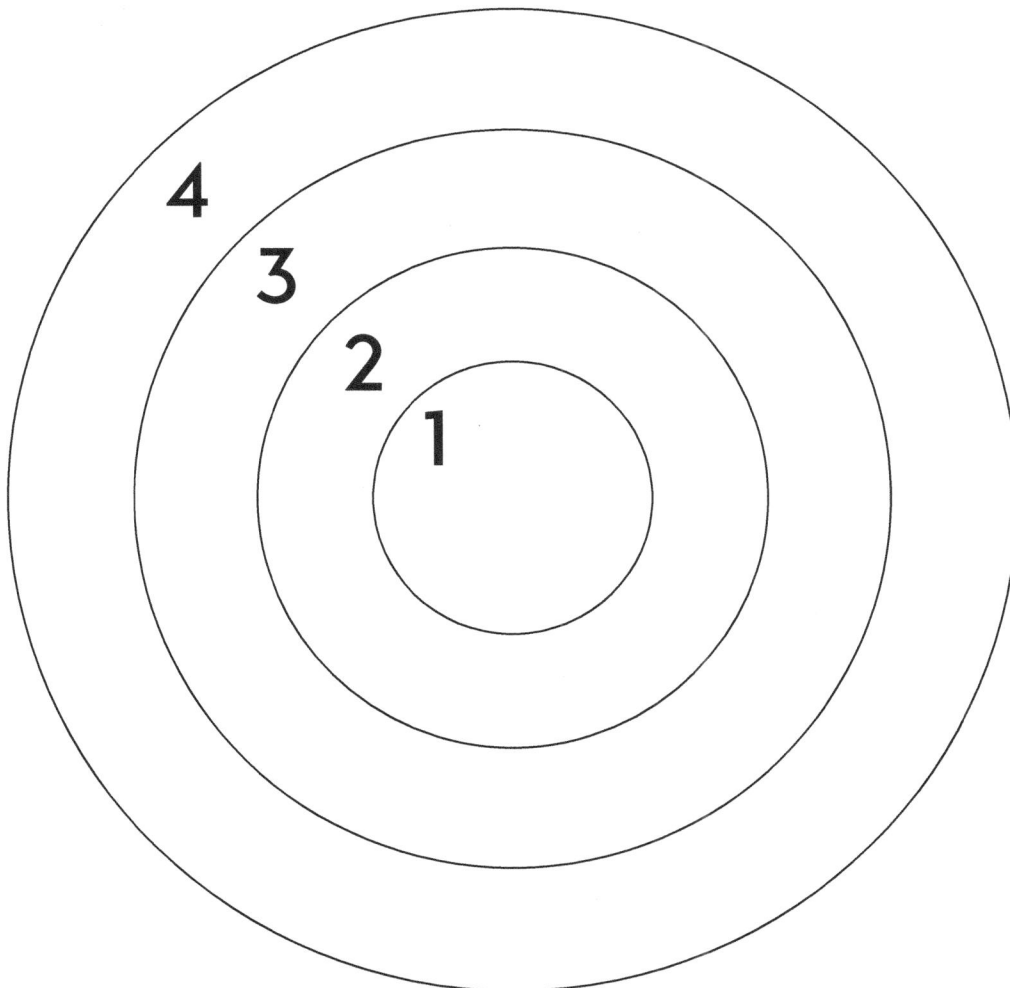

RACE: THE POWER OF AN ILLUSION

Note how the film answers these questions as you watch the clip from Episode 2: "The Story We Tell" of *Race: The Power of an Illusion*.

1. According to the video, how did the Founding Fathers explain the contradiction between their ideals of freedom and liberty and the existence of slavery in early America?

2. In 1619, when the first Africans arrived in Virginia, what defined social status? What types of differences had the most meaning?

3. Why did planters eventually identify Africans as the ideal labor source to enslave —better than indentured servants from Europe or Native Americans?

4. Why did whiteness become important to the identity of many Virginians? Why did being white become a more important characteristic than being Christian or English?

5. What gave white Americans the idea that Africans were "a different kind of people"?

6. What do we mean when we say that the idea of race is "socially constructed"?

EXCERPT FROM THE EMANCIPATION PROCLAMATION

That on the first day of January, in the year of our Lord one thousand eight hundred and sixty-three, all persons held as slaves within any State or designated part of a State, the people whereof shall then be in rebellion against the United States, shall be then, thenceforward, and forever free; and the Executive Government of the United States, including the military and naval authority thereof, will recognize and maintain the freedom of such persons, and will do no act or acts to repress such persons, or any of them, in any efforts they may make for their actual freedom.[1]

---

[1] Emancipation Proclamation, January 1, 1863 (excerpt); Presidential Proclamations, 1791–1991; Record Group 11; General Records of the United States Government; National Archives.

THE THIRTEENTH AMENDMENT

Section 1. Neither slavery nor involuntary servitude, except as a punishment for crime whereof the party shall have been duly convicted, shall exist within the United States, or any place subject to their jurisdiction.

Section 2. Congress shall have power to enforce this article by appropriate legislation.[1]

[1] US Const. amend. XII, § 1 and 2.

SAVANNAH FREEDPEOPLE EXPRESS THEIR ASPIRATIONS FOR FREEDOM

In January 1865, after Union general William T. Sherman's army arrived in Savannah, Georgia, followed by thousands of newly emancipated people, the secretary of war, Edwin Stanton, joined Sherman at a meeting with representatives of Savannah's Black community. The Black community chose Garrison Frazier, a minister who was formerly enslaved, to represent their views before Sherman and Stanton. What follows is an excerpt from the transcript of this meeting, known as the Savannah Colloquy. Following the meeting, Sherman ordered 400,000 acres of land along the coasts of South Carolina, Georgia, and Florida to be divided into 40-acre plots and given to freedpeople and their families.

1. State what your understanding is in regard to the acts of Congress, and President Lincoln's proclamation, touching the condition of the colored people in the rebel States.

Answer: So far as I understand President Lincoln's proclamation to the rebellious States, it is, that if they would lay down their arms and submit to the laws of the United States before the 1st of January, 1863, all should be well; but if they did not, then all the slaves in the rebel States should be free, henceforth and forever: that is what I understood.

2. State what you understand by slavery, and the freedom that was to be given by the President's Proclamation.

Answer: Slavery is receiving by irresistible power the work of another man, and not by his consent. The freedom, as I understand it, promised by the proclamation, is taking us from under the yoke of bondage and placing us where we could reap the fruit of our own labor, and take care of ourselves, and assist the Government in maintaining our freedom.

3. State in what manner you think you can take care of yourselves, and how can you best assist the Government in maintaining your freedom.

Answer: The way we can best take care of ourselves is to have land, and turn it and till it by our labor—that is, by the labor of the women, and children, and old men— and we can soon maintain ourselves and have something to spare . . . We want to be placed on land until we are able to buy it and make it our own.

4. State in what manner you would rather live, whether scattered among the whites, or in colonies by yourselves.

Answer: I would prefer to live by ourselves, for there is a prejudice against us in the South that will take years to get over; but I do not know that I can answer for my brethren.

[Mr. Lynch says he thinks they should not be separated, but live together. All the other persons present being questioned, one by one, answer that they agree with 'brother Frazier.']

5. Do you think that there is intelligence enough among the slaves of the South to maintain themselves under the Government of the United States, and the equal protection of its laws, and maintain good and peaceable relations among yourselves and with your neighbors?

Answer: I think there is sufficient intelligence among us to do so.[1]

[1] "Sherman Meets the Colored Ministers in Savannah," O.R. Series I, Vol. XLVII/2 [S# 99], Union Correspondence, Orders, and Returns Relating to Operations in North Carolina (from February 1), South Carolina, Southern Georgia, and east Florida, from January 1, 1865, to March 23, 1865, #2.

WHAT THE BLACK MAN WANTS

During the Reconstruction era, Frederick Douglass demanded government action to secure land, voting rights, and civil equality for Black Americans. The following passage is excerpted from a speech given by Douglass to the Massachusetts Anti-Slavery Society in April 1865.

We may be asked, I say, why we want it [the right to vote]. I will tell you why we want it. We want it because it is our *right*, first of all. No class of men can, without insulting their own nature, be content with any deprivation of their rights. We want it again, as a means for educating our race. Men are so constituted that they derive their conviction of their own possibilities largely from the estimate formed of them by others. If nothing is expected of a people, that people will find it difficult to contradict that expectation. By depriving us of suffrage, you affirm our incapacity to form an intelligent judgment respecting public men and public measures; you declare before the world that we are unfit to exercise the elective franchise, and by this means lead us to undervalue ourselves, to put a low estimate upon ourselves, and to feel that we have no possibilities like other men . . .

What I ask for the Negro is not benevolence, not pity, not sympathy, but simply *justice*. [Applause.] The American people have always been anxious to know what they shall do with us . . . everybody has asked the question, and they learned to ask it early of the abolitionists, "What shall we do with the Negro?" I have had but one answer from the beginning. Do nothing with us! . . . All I ask is, give him a chance to stand on his own legs! Let him alone! If you see him on his way to school, let him alone, don't disturb him! If you see him going to the dinner-table at a hotel, let him go! If you see him going to the ballot-box, let him alone, don't disturb him! . . .[1]

[1] Frederick Douglass, "What the Black Man Wants" (speech before the Massachusetts Anti-Slavery Society, April 1865), available at http://teachingamericanhistory.org/library/document/what-the-black-man-wants/ (accessed April 25, 2013).

LETTER FROM JOURDON ANDERSON: A FREEDMAN WRITES HIS FORMER MASTER

Dayton, Ohio, August 7, 1865.

To my old Master, Colonel P. H. Anderson, Big Spring, Tennessee.

Sir:

I got your letter, and was glad to find that you had not forgotten Jourdon, and that you wanted me to come back and live with you again, promising to do better for me than anybody else can. I have often felt uneasy about you. I thought the Yankees would have hung you long before this, for harboring Rebs they found at your house. I suppose they never heard about your going to Colonel Martin's to kill the Union soldier that was left by his company in their stable. Although you shot at me twice before I left you, I did not want to hear of your being hurt, and am glad you are still living. It would do me good to go back to the dear old home again, and see Miss Mary and Miss Martha and Allen, Esther, Green, and Lee. Give my love to them all, and tell them I hope we will meet in the better world, if not in this. I would have gone back to see you all when I was working in the Nashville Hospital, but one of the neighbors told me that Henry intended to shoot me if he ever got a chance.

I want to know particularly what the good chance is you propose to give me. I am doing tolerably well here. I get $25 a month, with victuals and clothing; have a comfortable home for Mandy (the folks call her Mrs. Anderson), and the children, Milly, Jane, and Grundy, go to school and are learning well. The teacher says Grundy has a head for a preacher. They go to Sunday school, and Mandy and me attend church regularly. We are kindly treated. Sometimes we overhear others saying, "Them colored people were slaves" down in Tennessee. The children feel hurt when they hear such remarks; but I tell them it was no disgrace in Tennessee to belong to Colonel Anderson. Many darkeys would have been proud, as I used to be, to call you master. Now if you will write and say what wages you will give me, I will be better able to decide whether it would be to my advantage to move back again.

As to my freedom, which you say I can have, there is nothing to be gained on that score, as I got my free papers in 1864 from the Provost-Marshal-General of the department of Nashville. Mandy says she would be afraid to go back without some proof that you were disposed to treat us justly and kindly; and we have concluded to test your sincerity by asking you to send us our wages for the time we served you. This will make us forget and forgive old scores, and rely on your justice and friendship in the future. I served you faithfully for thirty-two years, and Mandy twenty years. At $25 a month for me, and $2 a week for Mandy, our earnings would amount to $11,680. Add to this the interest for the time our wages have been kept back, and deduct what you paid for our clothing, and three doctor's visits to me, and pulling a tooth for Mandy, and the balance will show what we are in justice entitled to. Please send the money by Adams express, in care of V. Winters, esq., Dayton, Ohio. If you fail to pay us for faithful labors in the past, we can have little faith in your promises in the future. We trust the good Maker has opened your eyes to the wrongs which you and your fathers have done to me and my fathers, in making us toil for you for generations without recompense. Here I draw my wages every Saturday night; but in Tennessee there was never any pay-day for the negroes any more than for the horses and cows. Surely there will be a day of reckoning for those who defraud the laborer of his hire.

In answering this letter, please state if there would be any safety for my Milly and Jane, who are now grown up, and both good-looking girls. You know how it was with poor Matilda and Catherine. I would rather stay here and starve and die, if it come to that, than have my girls brought to shame by the violence and wickedness of their young masters. You will also please state if there has been any schools opened for the colored children in your neighborhood. The great desire of my life now is to give my children an education, and have them form virtuous habits.

From your old servant,

Jourdon Anderson

P.S.— Say howdy to George Carter, and thank him for taking the pistol from you when you were shooting at me.[1]

---

[1] Excerpted from William E. Gienapp, ed., *The Civil War and Reconstruction: A Documentary Collection* (New York: W. W. Norton, 2001), 380.

SOUTH CAROLINA FREEDPEOPLE DEMAND EDUCATION

In November 1865, a convention of freedmen met in Charleston, South Carolina, to demand new rights for African Americans. Foremost among their demands was education for their children. The convention issued the following resolution:

> *Whereas*, "Knowledge is power," and an educated and intelligent people can neither be held in, nor reduced to slavery; Therefore [be it] Resolved, That we will insist upon the establishment of good schools for the thorough education of our children throughout the State; that, to this end, we will contribute freely and liberally of our means, and will earnestly and persistently urge forward every measure calculated to elevate us to the rank of a wise, enlightened and Christian people. Resolved, That we solemnly urge the parents and guardians of the young and rising generation, by the sad recollection of our *forced* ignorance and degradation in the past, and by the bright and inspiring hopes of the future, to see that schools are at once established in every neighborhood; and when so established, to see to it that every child of proper age, is kept in regular attendance upon the same.[1]

[1] *Proceedings of the Colored People's Convention of the State of South Carolina, Held in Zion Church, Charleston, November 1865* (Charleston: South Carolina Leader Office, 1865), 23–26.

STATISTICS FROM THE WAR[1]

750,000	Total number of deaths from the Civil War[2]
504	Deaths per day during the Civil War
2.5	Approximate percentage of the American population that died during the Civil War
7,000,000	Number of Americans lost if 2.5% of the American population died in a war today
8,064	Number of American soldiers who died in the wars in Afghanistan and Iraq (as of 3/13/13)[3]
2,100,000	Number of Northerners mobilized to fight for the Union army
880,000	Number of Southerners mobilized to fight for the Confederacy
40+	Estimated percentage of Civil War dead who were never identified
66	Estimated percentage of dead African American Union soldiers who were never identified
2 out of 3	Number of Civil War deaths that occurred from disease rather than battle
68,162	Number of inquiries answered by the Missing Soldiers Office from 1865 to 1868
4,000,000	Number of enslaved persons in the United States in 1860
180,000	Number of African American soldiers that served in the Civil War
1 in 5	Average death rate for all Civil War soldiers
3:1	Ratio of Confederate deaths to Union deaths
9:1	Ratio of African American Civil War troops who died of disease to those that died on the battlefield, largely due to discriminatory medical care
100,000+	Number of Civil War Union corpses found in the South through a federal reinterment program from 1866 to 1869
303,356	Number of Union soldiers who were reinterred in 74 congressionally mandated national cemeteries by 1871
0	Number of Confederate soldiers buried in those national cemeteries

[1] Except where noted, figures adapted from "The Civil War by the Numbers," American Experience: *Death and the Civil War* companion website, http://www.pbs.org/wgbh/americanexperience/features/general-article/death-numbers/ (accessed April 25, 2013).

[2] Guy Gugliotta, "New Estimate Raises Civil War Death Toll," *New York Times*, April 3, 2012, http://www.nytimes.com/2012/04/03/science/civil-war-toll-up-by-20-percent-in-new-estimate.html.

[3] Iraq and Afghanistan statistics from http://www.cnn.com/SPECIALS/war.casualties/table.iraq.html.

A DAY OF TRIUMPH

The following is an excerpt from the diary of Caroline Barrett White (1828–1915), a resident of Brookline, Massachusetts.

Monday, April 10, 1865

Hurrah! Hurrah! . . . Early this morning our ears were greeted with the sound of bells ringing a joyous peal—& a paper sent home by Frank announced the glad tidings that Gen. Lee had surrendered with his whole Army to Gen. Grant! Surely "This is the Lord's doings, & it is marvelous in our eyes"—The city has been given up to rejoicings all day & this evening there was to have been a great illumination—with music fireworks & such other demonstrations as are usual in a time like this . . . April 9th! Will long be remembered as a day of triumph—just as one week ago came the thrilling intelligence of the fall of Petersburg & Richmond—& today the greater triumph still of the surrender of Gen. Lee of the Army of Northern Virginia—This crowns a week unparalleled in the annals of this war—& I doubt if a parallel could be found in all history . . . I wish I could be near to join in the general jubilation—it is stupid enough to be sitting alone in a quiet room—where only the faint echoes of a city's burst of joy reach me—Ah! Well! I can be grateful to the Lord who has made bare His Arm to save this people—& who has brought them through great tribulation— through sufferings not to be described—through battle fields, red with the blood of the best of their sons—to see this belled day—step by step has He led this people up even higher & higher— on to the great plans of righteousness—justice & freedom . . . I think we ought to know what patriotism means—and shall realize more fully than ever what it is to have a Country—and our children will have an inheritance greatly to be desired. Let our starry banner wave—from sea to sea and no slave shall look upon its glorious folds—no chains shall clank beneath it—but every where, & to all people, of every color shall it be the loved emblem of liberty.[1]

---

[1] Excerpted from *The Caroline Barrett White Papers, 1844–1915*, at the American Antiquarian Society (Worcester, MA).

CONQUERED

The following is an excerpt from the diary of Kate Stone (1841–1907), who fled to Texas from her family's plantation in Louisiana after the Union victory at Vicksburg.

May 15, 1865

Conquered, *Submission*, *Subjugation* are words that burn into my heart, and yet I feel that we are doomed to know them in all their bitterness. The war is rushing rapidly to a disastrous close. Another month and our Confederacy will be a Nation no longer, but we will be slaves, yes slaves, of the Yankee government.

The degradation seems more than we can bear. How can we bend our necks to the tyrants' yoke? Our glorious struggle of the last four years, our hardships, our sacrifices, and worst of all, the torrents of noble blood that have been shed for our loved Country—all, all in vain. The best and bravest of the South sacrificed—and for nothing. Yes, worse than nothing. Only to rivet more firmly the chains that bind us. The bitterness of death is in the thought. We could bear the loss of my brave little brothers when we thought that they had fallen at the post of duty defending their Country, but now to know that those glad, bright spirits suffered and toiled in vain, that the end is overwhelming defeat, the thought is unendurable. And we may never be allowed to raise a monument where their graves sadden the hillside. There is a gloom over all like the shadow of death. We have given up hope for our beloved Country and all are humiliated, crushed to the earth. A past of grief and hardship, a present of darkness and despair, and a future without hope. Truly our punishment is greater than we can bear.

Since Johnston's surrender the people in this department are hopeless. If we make a stand, it would only delay the inevitable with the loss of many valuable lives. The leaders say the country is too much disheartened to withstand the power of a victorious Yankee army flushed with victory. Still, many hope there will be a rally and one more desperate struggle for freedom. If we cannot gain independence, we might compel better terms.

By the twenty-fourth we will know our fate—Submission to the Union (how we hate the word!), Confiscation, and Negro equality—or a bloody unequal struggle to last we know not how long. God help us, for vain is the help of man.[1]

---

[1] Excerpted from John Q. Anderson, ed., *Brokenburn: The Journal of Kate Stone (1861–1868)* (Baton Rouge: Louisiana State University Press, 1955), 339–40, https://archive.org/details/brokenburnthejou008676mbp.

REACTIONS TO LINCOLN'S ASSASSINATION

CAROLINE BARRETT WHITE:

Saturday, April 15, 1865

The darkest day I ever remember—This morning the sun rose upon a nation jubilant with victory—but it sets upon one plunged in deepest sorrow . . . midday—came the shocking intelligence that our beloved President Abraham Lincoln was dead—shot by a brutal assassin— last evening—as he was sitting cheerfully chatting with his wife & other friends in a box at the theatre—he lingered unconscious till about eight o'clock this morning—& died without a word or sign . . . later in the day came rumors of having secured the murderer—who it is affirmed by Miss Laura Keeve to be J. Wilkes Booth; oh! Where will treason end? & What shall we do with such as fall into our hands . . . The rapidity with which events crowd upon one another is perfectly bewildering. Frank is away & it (?) hard to be alone . . . When will our cup of punishments be drunk to the dregs? Merciful father, help us.[1]

KATE STONE:

April 28, 1865

We hear that Lincoln is dead. There can be no doubt, I suppose, that he has been killed by J. W. Booth. "*Sic semper tyrannis*" as his brave destroyer shouted as he sprang on his horse. All honor to J. Wilkes Booth, who has rid the world of a tyrant and made himself famous for generations. Surratt has also won the love and applause of all Southerners by his daring attack on Seward, whose life is trembling in the balance. How earnestly we hope our two avengers may escape to the South where they will meet with a warm welcome. It is a terrible tragedy, but what is war but one long tragedy? What torrents of blood Lincoln has caused to flow, and how Seward has aided him in his bloody work. I cannot be sorry for their fate. They deserve it. They have reaped their just reward.[2]

---

[1] Excerpted from *The Caroline Barrett White Papers, 1844–1915*, at the American Antiquarian Society (Worcester, MA).

[2] Excerpted from John Q. Anderson, ed., *Brokenburn: The Journal of Kate Stone (1861–1868)* (Baton Rouge: Louisiana State University Press, 1955), 333, https://archive.org/details/brokenburnthejou008676mbp.

HEALING AND JUSTICE

Read the statement in the left column. Decide if you strongly agree (**SA**), agree (**A**), disagree (**D**), or strongly disagree (**SD**) with it. Circle your response and provide a one- to two-sentence explanation of your opinion (on separate paper if needed).

STATEMENT	YOUR OPINION			
1. Those who win a war have the right to impose any punishment they wish on those who lost.	SA A D SD Explain:			
2. Allowing former Confederates to vote, hold office, and resume governing their states (but without slavery) is the quickest way to restore the Union and heal the hatreds that caused the Civil War.	SA A D SD Explain:			
3. During and after the Civil War, the federal government had the right to seize land owned by Southern planters and give it to freedpeople.	SA A D SD Explain:			
4. To ensure the strongest possible democracy after the Civil War, neither former slaves nor former Confederates should be excluded from voting and holding office.	SA A D SD Explain:			

STATEMENT	YOUR OPINION
5. Forcing ex-Confederates to take an oath in support of the United States and the Constitution is an effective way to ensure that they will accept the end of slavery and be loyal citizens.	SA A D SD Explain:
6. Giving freedpeople citizenship, voting rights, and the ability to hold elected office would not be worth it if such steps make it difficult for healing to occur between the North and South.	SA A D SD Explain:

CREATING A PLAN FOR RECONSTRUCTION

Create a proposal for a plan for Reconstruction after the Civil War. Your plan should seek to achieve two goals:

> 1. To reunite the nation, resolve the conflicts that led to the Civil War, and heal the wounds the war caused, and

> 2. To bring justice to the nation and its citizens.

Your plan should address each of the following dilemmas that the United States faced as the Civil War ended:

> 1. What will happen to each of the groups of ex-Confederates listed below? Will they be citizens? Will they be permitted to vote? Will they be permitted to hold office in the government?

>> • Confederate leaders (government officials/military officers)

>> • Wealthy, slave-owning planters

>> • Women who ran plantation households

>> • Low-ranking soldiers

>> • Working-class and poor whites

> 2. What will happen to freedpeople and other African Americans? Will they be citizens? Will they be permitted to vote and hold office? What other rights will they be provided?

> 3. What will happen to the land and other property confiscated by the Union army or abandoned during the war? Who has the right to use it? Who has the right to own it?

> 4. What is the best way to ensure that white Southerners will be loyal to the United States and accept the end of slavery?

After you have created a plan that addresses the dilemmas above, evaluate it by answering these questions:

> • Who are the winners and losers in your plan?

> • How will your plan help to reunite and heal the country?

> • How will your plan bring about justice after the war? Does it deny justice to any group of Americans?

FREEDPEOPLE PROTEST THE LOSS OF THEIR LAND

In January 1865, General Sherman acted on the testimony of the freedpeople of Savannah, Georgia, by issuing Special Field Order 15. The field order divided up land abandoned by Southern planters along the coasts of South Carolina, Georgia, and Florida and gave it to freedpeople in 40-acre plots. Under President Johnson's Reconstruction policies, most of that land was taken from the freedpeople and returned to its original owners later that year. The following is a letter from the Committee of Freedmen on Edisto Island, South Carolina, to Freedmen's Bureau Commissioner O. O. Howard responding to Johnson's land policy.

[*Edisto Island, S.C., October 20 or 21, 1865*]

General It Is with painfull Hearts that we the committe address you, we Have thorougholy considered the order which you wished us to Sighn, we wish we could do so but cannot feel our rights Safe If we do so,

General we want Homestead's; we were promised Homestead's by the government, If It does not carry out the promises Its agents made to us, If the government Haveing concluded to befriend Its late enemies and to neglect to observe the principles of common faith between Its self and us Its allies In the war you said was over, now takes away from them all right to the soil they stand upon save such as they can get by again working for *your* late and thier *all time ememies*.—If the government does so we are left In a more unpleasant condition than our former

we are at the mercy of those who are combined to prevent us from getting land enough to lay our fathers bones upon. We Have property In Horses, cattle, carriages, & articles of furniture, but we are landless and Homeless, from the Homes we Have lived In In the past we can only do one of three things Step Into the public *road or the sea* or remain on them working as In former time and subject to thire will as then. We cannot resist It In any way without being driven out Homeless upon the road.

You will see this Is not the condition of really freemen

You ask us to forgive the land owners of our Island, *You* only lost your right arm. In war and might forgive them. The man who tied me to a tree & gave me 39 lashes & who stripped and flogged my mother & my sister & who will not let me stay In His empty Hut except I will do His planting & be Satisfied with His price & who combines with others to keep away land from me well knowing I would not Have any thing to do with Him If I Had land of my own.—that man, I cannot well forgive. Does It look as If He Has forgiven me, seeing How He tries to keep me In a condition of Helplessness

General, we cannot remain Here In such condition and If the government permits them to come back we ask It to Help us to reach land where we shall not be slaves nor compelled to work for those who would treat us as such

we Have not been treacherous, we Have not for selfish motives allied to us those who suffered like us from a common enemy & then Haveing gained *our* purpose left our allies In thier Hands There Is no rights secured to us there Is no law likely to be made which our Hands can reach. The state will make laws that we shall not be able to Hold land even If we pay for It landless, Homeless. Voteless. we can only pray to god & Hope for *His Help, your Infuence & assistance* With consideration of esteem your

Obt Servts
In behalf of the people

Henry
Bram Committe Ishmael
Moultrie
yates Sampson[1]

[1] Published in Stephen Hahn et al., eds., *Land and Labor, 1865* (*Freedom: A Documentary History of Emancipation, 1861–1867*, Series 3, vol. 1) (University of North Carolina Press, 2008), available at http://www.history.umd.edu/freedmen/Edisto%20petitions.htm.

A RIGHT TO THE LAND

In 1866, after army officials forced freedman Bayley Wyatt to vacate the Virginia land he had occupied since the end of the war, he argued at a public meeting for freedpeople's right to the land as follows:

> We now, as a people desires to be elevated, and we desires to do all we can to be educated, and we hope our friends will aid us all they can . . .

> I may state to all our friends, and to all our enemies, that we has a right to the land where we are located. For why? I tell you. Our wives, our children, our husbands, has been sold over and over again to purchase the lands we now locate upon; for that reason we have a divine right to the land . . .

> And then didn't we clear the land and raise the crops of corn, of cotton, of tobacco, of rice, of sugar, of everything? And then didn't them large cities in the North grow up on the cotton and the sugars and the rice that we made? Yes! I appeal to the South and the North if I hasn't spoken the words of truth. I say they have grown rich, and my people is poor.[1]

---

[1] From Roy E. Finkenbine, *Sources of the African-American Past: Primary Sources in American History*, 2nd ed. (Pearson, 2003), 88.

SHARECROPPING CONTRACT

[December 23, 1865]

Thomas J. Ross agrees to employ the said freedmen to plant and raise a crop on his Rosstown Plantation for the year 1866 in Shelby County, Tenn. on the following Rules, Regulations and Renumerations.

. . . Ross agrees to furnish the land to cultivate, and a sufficient number of mules & horses and feed them to make and house said crop and all necessary farming utensils to carry on the same and to give unto said freedmen whose names appear below one half of all the cotton, corn and wheat that is raised there for the year 1866 after all the necessary expenses are deducted . . .

. . . And we the said freedmen agrees to furnish ourselves & families in provisions, clothing, medicine and medical bills and all, and every kind of other expenses that we may incur on the plantation for the year 1866 free of charge to said Ross. Should the said Ross furnish us any of the above supplies or any other kind of expenses, during said year, we are to settle and pay him out of the nett proceeds of our part of the crop the retail price of the county at time of sale or any price we may agree upon—The said Ross shall keep a regular book account . . . to be adjusted and settled at the end of the year . . .

We furthermore bind ourselves to and with said Ross that we will do good work and labor ten hours a day on an average, winter and summer . . . The time we are going to and from work shall not be computed or counted in the time . . . We further agree that we will loose all lost time, or pay at the rate of one dollar per day, rainy days excepted . . .

We furthermore bind ourselves that we will obey the orders of Ross in all things in carrying out and managing the crop for the year and further bind ourselves that we said freedmen will keep up the fences around the enclosures, and lots especially and if any rails be missing by burning or otherwise destroyed by said freedmen, we will pay for them or otherwise reconstruct the fence anew at our expense . . .

All is responsible for all farming utensils that is on hand or may be placed in care of said freedmen for the year 1866 to said Ross and are also responsible to said Ross if we carelessly, maliciously maltreat any of his stock for said year to said Ross for damages to be assessed out of our wages for said year, all of which is understood by us freedmen in the foregoing contract, or agreement, Ross assigning his name and ours following. It is further agreed by us whose names appear below that we will keep a sufficiency of firewood hawled up at all times and make fires in the room of Ross, when desired, attend to all stock properly, under direction of said Ross . . . .[1]

---

[1] Excerpted from records at *The Freedmen's Bureau Online*, http://freedmensbureau.com/tennessee/contracts/miscellaneouscontracts.htm.

HE WAS ALWAYS RIGHT AND YOU WERE ALWAYS WRONG

Henry Blake, a freedman from Arkansas, describes how sharecropping limited his freedom in these words:

> When we worked on shares, we couldn't make nothing, just overalls and something to eat. Half went to the other man and you would destroy your half, if you weren't careful. A man that didn't know how to count would always lose. He might lose anyhow. They didn't give no itemized statement. No, you just had to take their word. They never give you no details. No matter how good account you kept, you had to go by their account, and now, Brother, I'm tellin' you the truth about this. It's been that way for a long time. You had to take the white man's work on note, and everything. Anything you wanted, you could git if you were a good hand. You could git anything you wanted as long as you worked. If you didn't make no money, that's all right; they would advance you more. But you better not leave him, you better not try to leave and get caught. They'd keep you in debt. They were sharp. Christmas come, you could take up twenty dollar, in somethin' to eat and as much as you wanted in whiskey. You could buy a gallon of whiskey. Anything that kept you a slave because he was always right and you were always wrong if there was a difference. If there was an argument, he would get mad and there would be a shooting take place.[1]

[1] From *Henry Blake, Little Rock, Arkansas*, Federal Writers' Project, US Work Projects Administration (Manuscript Division), Library of Congress, available at the *History Matters* website, http://historymatters.gmu.edu/d/6377/.

MISSISSIPPI BLACK CODES (1865)

CIVIL RIGHTS OF FREEDMEN

Section 3: . . . [I]t shall not be lawful for any freedman, free negro or mulatto to intermarry with any white person; nor for any person to intermarry with any freedman, free negro or mulatto; and any person who shall so intermarry shall be deemed guilty of felony, and on conviction thereof shall be confined in the State penitentiary for life; and those shall be deemed freedmen, free negroes and mulattoes who are of pure negro blood, and those descended from a negro to the third generation, inclusive, though one ancestor in each generation may have been a white person.

Section 5: . . . Every freedman, free negro and mulatto shall, on the second Monday of January, one thousand eight hundred and sixty-six, and annually thereafter, have a lawful home or employment, and shall have written evidence thereof . . .

Section 6: . . . All contracts for labor made with freedmen, free negroes and mulattoes for a longer period than one month shall be in writing, and a duplicate, attested and read to said freedman, free negro or mulatto by a beat, city or county officer . . . and if the laborer shall quit the service of the employer before the expiration of his term of service, without good cause, he shall forfeit his wages for that year up to the time of quitting.

Section 7: . . . Every civil officer shall, and every person may, arrest and carry back to his or her legal employer any freedman, free negro, or mulatto who shall have quit the service of his or her employer before the expiration of his or her term of service without good cause . . .

VAGRANT LAW

Section 1: . . . That all rogues and vagabonds, idle and dissipated persons, beggars, jugglers, or persons practicing unlawful games or plays, runaways, common drunkards, common night-walkers, pilferers, lewd, wanton, or lascivious persons, in speech or behavior, common railers and brawlers, persons who neglect their calling or employment, misspend what they earn, or do not provide for the support of themselves or their families, or dependents, and all other idle and disorderly persons, including all who neglect all lawful business, habitually misspend their time by frequenting houses of ill-fame, gaming-houses, or tippling shops, shall be deemed and considered vagrants, under the provisions of this act, and upon conviction thereof shall be fined not exceeding one hundred dollars, with all accruing costs, and be imprisoned, at the discretion of the court, not exceeding ten days.

Section 2: . . . All freedmen, free negroes and mulattoes in this State, over the age of eighteen years, found on the second Monday in January, 1866, or thereafter, with no lawful employment or business, or found unlawful assembling themselves together, either in the day or night time, and all white persons assembling themselves with freedmen, free negroes or mulattoes, or usually associating with freedmen, free negroes or mulattoes, on terms of equality, or living in adultery or fornication with a freed woman, freed negro or mulatto, shall be deemed vagrants, and on conviction thereof shall be fixed in a sum not exceeding, in the case of a freedman, free negro or mulatto, fifty dollars, and a white man two hundred dollars, and imprisonment at the discretion of the court, the free negro not exceeding ten days, and the white man not exceeding six months . . .

Section 5: . . . All fines and forfeitures collected by the provisions of this act shall be paid into the county treasury of general county purposes, and in case of any freedman, free negro or mulatto shall fail for five days after the imposition of any or forfeiture upon him or her for violation of any of the provisions of this act to pay the same, that it shall be, and is hereby, made the duty of the sheriff of the proper county to hire out said freedman, free negro or mulatto, to any person who will, for the shortest period of service, pay said five and forfeiture and all costs . . .

CERTAIN OFFENSES OF FREEDMEN

Section 1: . . . That no freedman, free negro or mulatto, not in the military service of the United States government, and not licensed so to do by the board of police of his or her county, shall keep or carry fire-arms of any kind, or any ammunition, dirk or bowie knife, and on conviction thereof in the county court shall be punished by fine . . .

Section 2: . . . Any freedman, free negro, or mulatto committing riots, routs, affrays, trespasses, malicious mischief, cruel treatment to animals, seditious speeches, insulting gestures, language, or acts, or assaults on any person, disturbance of the peace, exercising the function of a minister of the gospel without a license from some regularly organized church, vending spirituous or intoxicating liquors, or committing any other misdemeanor, the punishment of which is not specifically provided for by law, shall, upon conviction thereof in the county court, be fined not less than ten dollars, and not more than one hundred dollars, and may be imprisoned at the discretion of the court, not exceeding thirty days.

Section 3: . . . If any white person shall sell, lend, or give to any freedman, free negro, or mulatto any fire-arms, dirk or bowie knife, or ammunition, or any spirituous or intoxicating liquors, such person or persons so offending, upon conviction thereof in the county court of his or her county, shall be fined not exceeding fifty dollars, and may be imprisoned, at the discretion of the court, not exceeding thirty days . . .

---

[1] Excerpted from William E. Gienapp, ed., *The Civil War and Reconstruction: A Documentary Collection* (New York: W. W. Norton, 2001), 325.

FREEDMEN'S BUREAU AGENT REPORTS ON PROGRESS IN EDUCATION

The following is an excerpt from a January 1866 Freedmen's Bureau report on education for freedpeople in the South, written by Freedmen's Bureau inspector John W. Alvord.

Not only are individuals seen at study, and under the most untoward circumstances, but in very many places I have found what I will call "native schools," often rude and very imperfect, *but there they are*, a group, perhaps, of all ages, *trying to learn*. Some young man, some woman, or old preacher, in cellar, or shed, or corner of a negro meeting-house, with the alphabet in hand, or a torn spelling-book, is their teacher. All are full of enthusiasm with the new knowledge The Book is imparting to them . . .

A still higher order of this native teaching is seen in the colored schools at Charleston, Savannah, and New Orleans. With many disadvantages they bear a very good examination. One I visited in the latter city, of 300 pupils, and wholly taught by educated colored men, would bear comparison with any ordinary school at the north. Not only good reading and spelling were heard, but lessons at the black-board in arithmetic, recitations in geography and English grammar. Very creditable specimens of writing were shown, and all the older classes could read or recite as fluently in French as in English. There was a free school, wholly supported by the colored people of the city . . . All the above cases illustrate the remark that this educational movement among the freedmen has in it a self-sustaining element. I took special pains to ascertain the facts on this particular point, and have to report that there are schools of this kind in some stage of advancement (taught and supported wholly by the people themselves) in all the large places I visited—often *numbers* of them, and they are also making their appearance through the *interior* of the entire country. The superintendent of South Carolina assured me that there was not a place of any size in the whole of that State where such a school was not attempted. I have much testimony, both oral and written, from others well informed, that the same is true of other States. There can scarcely be a doubt, and I venture the estimate, that at least 500 schools of this description are already in operation throughout the south. If, therefore, all these be added, and including soldiers and individuals at study, we shall have at least 125,000 as the *entire educational census of this lately emancipated people*.

This is a wonderful state of things. We have just emerged from a terrific war; peace is not yet declared. There is scarcely the beginning of reorganized society at the south; and yet here is a people long imbruted by slavery, and the most despised of any on earth, whose chains are no sooner broken than they spring to their feet and start up an exceeding great army, clothing themselves with intelligence. What other people on earth have ever shown, while in their ignorance, such a passion for education?[1]

[1] United States Bureau of Refugees, Freedmen, and Abandoned Lands and John W. Alvord, *Freedmen's Schools and Textbooks, vol. 1, Semi-annual report on schools for freedmen: numbers 1–10, January 1866–July 1870* (AMS Press, 1868), 1–10.

THE FOURTEENTH AMENDMENT

The following Constitutional amendment was approved by Congress on June 13, 1866, and ratified on July 9, 1868.

Section 1. All persons born or naturalized in the United States, and subject to the jurisdiction thereof, are citizens of the United States and of the State wherein they reside. No State shall make or enforce any law which shall abridge the privileges or immunities of citizens of the United States; nor shall any State deprive any person of life, liberty, or property, without due process of law; nor deny to any person within its jurisdiction the equal protection of the laws.

Section 2. Representatives shall be apportioned among the several States according to their respective numbers, counting the whole number of persons in each State, excluding Indians not taxed.[1] But when the right to vote at any election for the choice of electors for President and Vice-President of the United States, representatives in Congress, the executive and judicial officers of a State, or the members of the legislature thereof, is denied to any of the male inhabitants of such State, being twenty-one years of age, and citizens of the United States, or in any way abridged, except for participation in rebellion, or other crime, the basis of representation therein shall be reduced in the proportion which the number of such male citizens shall bear to the whole number of male citizens twenty-one years of age in such State.

Section 3. No person shall be a senator, or representative in Congress, or elector of President and Vice-President, or hold any office, civil or military, under the United States, or under any State, who having previously taken an oath, as a member of Congress, or as an officer of the United States, or as a member of any State legislature, or as an executive or judicial officer of any State, to support the Constitution of the United States, shall have engaged in insurrection or rebellion against the same, or given aid or comfort to the enemies thereof. But Congress may by a vote of two-thirds of each House remove such disability.

Section 4. The validity of the public debt of the United States, authorized by law, including debts incurred for payment of pensions and bounties for services in suppressing insurrection or rebellion, shall not be questioned. But neither the United States nor any State shall assume or pay any debt or obligation incurred in aid of insurrection or rebellion against the United States, or any claim for the loss or emancipation of any slave; but all such debts, obligations, and claims shall be held illegal and void.

Section 5. The Congress shall have the power to enforce, by appropriate legislation, the provisions of this article.

---

[1] The phrase "Indians not taxed" appears in several laws and articles of the Constitution. American Indian tribes were considered "sovereign dependent nations" with their own governments. As a result, those who lived on Indian reservations or in unsettled US territories were not subject to state or federal taxes and did not count toward population totals used to determine representation in Congress. Until 1924, Native Americans born on reservations were not automatically citizens.

[2] Constitution of the United States, Amendment XIV, Sections 1–5.
Text available at http://memory.loc.gov/cgi-bin/ampage?collId=llsl&fileName=014/llsl014.db&recNum=389.

CONGRESS DEBATES THE FOURTEENTH AMENDMENT

GENERAL STATEMENTS:[1]

Rep. Eben Ingersoll (Republican from Illinois) comments on the potential of the amendment to change the nation:

"Carry out the policy of Andrew Johnson, and you will restore the old order of things, if the Government is not entirely destroyed: you will have the same old slave power, the enemy of liberty and justice, ruling this nation again, which ruled it for so many years."

Scholar Garrett Epps describes the Democratic Party's argument against the amendment:

"They dismissed the amendment as a useless contraption designed only for temporary partisan advantage; at the same time, they warned that the measure would transform the nation into a centralized despotism."

Senator Luke Poland (Republican from Vermont) comments on the difference he expects the amendment will make:

"[The South] will be opened and expanded by the influence of free labor and free institutions . . . All causes of discord between North and South being over, we shall become a homogeneous nation of freemen, dwelling together in peace and unity."

Senator Edgar Cowan (Democrat from Pennsylvania) comments on how the amendment will expand federal power:

"What conceivable difference could it make to a citizen of Pennsylvania as to how Ohio distributes her political power? . . . To touch, to venture upon that ground is to revolutionize the whole frame and texture of the system of our government."

Rep. Thaddeus Stevens (Republican from Pennsylvania) comments on the compromises in the amendment:

"Do you inquire why, holding these views and possessing some will of my own, I accept so imperfect a proposition? I answer, because I live among men and not among angels; among men as intelligent, as determined, and as independent as myself, who, not agreeing with me, do not choose to yield their opinions to mine. Mutual concession, therefore, is our only resort, or mutual hostilities."

SECTION 1:

Rep. Thaddeus Stevens (Republican from Pennsylvania) comments on Section 1:

"[Section 1] allows Congress to correct the unjust legislation of the states, so far that the law which operates upon one man shall operate equally upon all. Whatever law punishes a white man for a crime shall punish the black man precisely in the same way and to the same degree. Whatever law protects the white man shall afford 'equal protection' to the black man."

Scholar Garrett Epps describes Democratic opposition to Section 1:

"Andrew Rogers of New Jersey gave the fullest explanation of the opposition when he warned that the first section would take away the government's traditional power to choose groups among citizens who are worthy of 'privileges and immunities,' and would instead confer these treasured prerogatives as rights on the unworthy. 'The right to vote is a privilege,' he said. 'The right to marry is a privilege. The right to contract is a privilege. The right to be a juror is a privilege. The right to be a judge or President of United States is a privilege. I hold if [Section 1] ever becomes a part of the fundamental law of the land it will prevent any state from refusing to allow anything to anybody embraced under this term of privileges and immunities,' he said. 'That, sir, will be an introduction to the time when despotism and tyranny will march forth undisturbed and unbroken, in silence and in darkness, in this land which was once the land of freedom . . .'"

Senator Jacob Howard (Republican from Michigan) comments on Section 1:

"[Section 1] will, if adopted by the states, forever disable every one of them from passing laws trenching upon those fundamental rights and privileges which pertain to citizens of the United States, and to all persons who may happen to be within their jurisdiction. It establishes equality before the law, and it gives to the humblest, the poorest, the most despised of the race the same rights and the same protection before the law as it gives to the most powerful, the most wealthy, or the most haughty. That, sir, is republican government, as I understand it, and the only one which can claim the praise of a just Government."

Scholar Garrett Epps describes the impact of the amendment's definitions of citizenship:

"Nearly a century and a half later, the citizenship language seems almost obvious. But in 1866, the idea of a preeminent national citizenship was a radical repudiation of the 'state sovereignty' theory, which held that each state had a right to define its own qualifications for citizenship, and that Americans were state citizens first and only secondarily citizens of the Union. Edgar Cowan of Pennsylvania spoke for the Democrats in repudiating the radical implications of the new language, which would make both the nation and each state within it into multiracial republics, in which equality was a birthright and not a gift of the majority. The language, he said in horror, would make citizens of even the most undesirable nomads."

Senator Edgar Cowan (Democrat from Pennsylvania) warns about the ramifications of the amendment's definition of citizenship:

"There is a race in contact with this country which, in all characteristic except that of simply making fierce war, is not only our equal but perhaps our superior. I mean the yellow race; the Mongol race. They outnumber us largely. Of their industry, their skill, and their pertinacity in all worldly affairs, nobody can doubt . . . They may pour in their millions upon our Pacific Coast in a very short time.

Are the states to lose control over this immigration? Is the United States to determine that they are to be citizens?"

SECTION 2:

Scholar Garrett Epps describes Thaddeus Stevens's support for Section 2:

"To Stevens . . . the second section was 'the most important in the article,' because it would 'either compel the states to grant universal suffrage or so . . . shear them of their power as to keep them forever in a hopeless minority in the national Government.'"

Scholar Garrett Epps describes Senator Jacob Howard's (Republican from Michigan) support for Section 2:

"'[I favor black suffrage] to some extent at least, for I am opposed to the exclusion and proscription of an entire race.' But the committee did not believe a suffrage amendment could be ratified. So the second section 'is so drawn as to make it the political interest of the once slaveholding States to admit their colored population to the right of suffrage.' It would operate whether the Southern states drew a racial line to exclude freed slaves from voting or used a formally nonracial category like a literacy test, he said."

Rep. James Brooks (Democrat from New York) responds to the exclusion of women from Section 2:

"I raise my voice here on behalf of 15 million of our countrywomen, the fairest, brightest portion of creation, and I ask why they are not permitted to be represented under this resolution . . . Why, in organizing a system of liberality and justice, not recognize in the case of free women as well as free negroes the right of representation?"[2]

SECTION 3:

Scholar Garrett Epps describes revisions made to Section 3 during the debate in the Senate, changing the penalties for former Confederates:[3]

"The Senate unanimously struck out Section 3, which would have disenfranchised former Confederates from voting until 1870 . . . [Senator] Howard brought forward a new disenfranchisement section, far more lenient than the [previous] House version; it did not limit ex-Confederates' right to vote, but only excluded a small group from holding office: those who had 'previously taken an oath' to support the U.S. Constitution and then had afterward participated in the Confederate cause."

Historian Eric Foner describes the level of support for disenfranchising former Confederates:

"[A] majority of Republicans considered disenfranchisement [of former Confederates until 1870] vindictive, undemocratic, and likely to arouse opposition in the north."

SECTION 5:

Senator Jacob Howard (Republican from Michigan) comments on Section 5:

"[Section 5] casts upon Congress the responsibility of seeing to it, for the future, that all the sections of the amendment are carried out in good faith, and that no State infringes the rights of persons or property . . . It enables Congress, in case the States shall enact laws in conflict with the principles of the amendment, to correct that legislation by a formal congressional enactment."

Sen. Thomas Hendricks (Democrat from Indiana) comments on Section 5:

"When these words were used in the amendment abolishing slavery they were thought to be harmless; but during the session there has been claimed for them such force and scope of meaning as that Congress might invade the jurisdiction of the States, rob them of their reserved rights, and crown the Federal Government with absolute and despotic power."

---

[1] Except where noted, all quotations excerpted from Garrett Epps, *Democracy Reborn: The Fourteenth Amendment and the Fight for Equal Rights in Post-Civil War America* (Henry Holt, 2006), 224–39.

[2] Epps, *Democracy Reborn*, 111.

[3] Eric Foner, *Reconstruction: America's Unfinished Revolution, 1863–1877,* Perennial Classics ed. (HarperCollins, 2002), 254.

BLACK OFFICEHOLDERS IN THE SOUTH

The following seven tables provide information about the numbers of African American officeholders in the South during Reconstruction and the backgrounds of those officeholders.[1]

TABLE 1: Black Officeholders during Reconstruction by State	
Alabama	173
Arkansas	46
District of Columbia	11
Florida	58
Georgia	135
Louisiana	210
Mississippi	226
Missouri	1
North Carolina	187
South Carolina	316
Tennessee	20
Texas	49
Virginia	85
TOTAL	1,510*

* Historians estimate the total number of Black officeholders is closer to 2,000, but these numbers reflect only those for whom definite records exist.

TABLE 2: Black Officeholders during Reconstruction: Federal	
Ambassador	2
Census Marshal	6
Census Taker	14
Clerk	12
Congressman: Senate	2
Congressman: House of Representatives	14
Customs Appointment	40
Deputy US Marshal	11
Engineer	1
Mail Agent	14
Pensions Agent	1
Postmaster/Post Office Official	43
Register of Bankruptcy	1
Timber Agent	1
US Assessor	10
US Grand Jury	3
US Land Office	5
US Treasury Agent	3
Unidentified Patronage Appointment	2

[1] All data adapted from Eric Foner, *Freedom's Lawmakers: A Directory of Black Officeholders during Reconstruction*, revised ed. (Baton Rouge, LA: Louisiana State University Press, 1996), xi–xxxii.

TABLE 3: Black Members of Congress during Reconstruction

Alabama
Jeremiah Haralson
James T. Rapier
Benjamin S. Turner

Florida
Josiah T. Walls

Georgia
Jefferson Long

Louisiana
Charles E. Nash

Mississippi
Blanche K. Bruce*
John R. Lynch
Hiram Revels*

North Carolina
John A. Hyman

South Carolina
Richard H. Cain
Robert C. DeLarge
Robert B. Elliott
Joseph H. Rainey
Alonzo J. Ransier
Robert Smalls

* Served in US Senate

TABLE 4: Black Officeholders during Reconstruction: State

Assistant Commissioner of Agriculture	1
Assistant Secretary of State	3
Assistant Superintendent of Education	2
Board of Education	1
Constitutional Convention 1867–69: Delegate	267
Constitutional Convention 1875: Delegate (North Carolina)	7
Deaf and Dumb Asylum, Superintendent	1
Governor	1
Justice of Supreme Court	1
Land Commission, including County Agents (South Carolina)	10
Legislative Clerk	7
Legislator: House of Representatives	683
Legislator: Senate	112
Lieutenant Governor	6
Lunatic Asylum, Assistant Physician	1
Lunatic Asylum, Board of Regents	7
Militia Officer	60
Orphan Asylum, Board of Trustees	6
Secretary of State	9
Speaker of House	4
State Commissioner	5
Superintendent of Education	4
Treasurer	2

TABLE 5: Major Black State Officials during Reconstruction

Governor

Louisiana

P. B. S. Pinchback

Lieutenant Governor

Louisiana

Caesar C. Antoine
Oscar J. Dunn
P. B. S. Pinchback

Mississippi

Alexander K. Davis

South Carolina

Richard H. Cleaves
Alonzo J. Ransier

Treasurer

Louisiana

Antoine Dubuclet
South Carolina
Francis L. Cardozo

Superintendent of Education

Arkansas

Joseph C. Corbin

Florida

Jonathan C. Gibbs

Louisiana

William G. Brown

Mississippi

Thomas C. Cardozo

Speaker of the House

Mississippi

John R. Lynch
Isaac D. Shadd

South Carolina

Robert B. Elliott
Samuel J. Lee

Supreme Court

South Carolina

Jonathan J. Wright

State Commissioner

Arkansas

William H. Grey,
*Commr. of Immigration
and State Lands*

James T. White,
Commr. of Public Works

Mississippi

Richard Griggs,
*Commr. of Immigration
and Agriculture*

South Carolina

Robert G. DeLarge,
Land Commr.

Henry E. Hayne,
Land Commr.

TABLE 6: Black Officeholders during Reconstruction: County or Local

Assessor	32	Harbor Master	3
Auditor	7	Health Officer	1
Board of Education	79	Inspector	10
Board of Health	1	Jailor	9
Chancery Clerk	1	Judge	11
Charitable Institutions, Supervisor of	1	Jury Commissioner	1
City Attorney	1	Justice of the Peace or Magistrate	232
City Clerk	1	Lumber Measurer	1
City Council	146	Mayor	5
City Marshal	7	Notary Public	5
City Office (unidentified)	3	Ordinary	3
City Public Works Commissioner	2	Overseer of Poor	7
Claims Commissioner	1	Overseer of Roads	1
Clerk	12	Park Commissioner	1
Clerk of Court	24	Police Officer	71
Clerk of Market	2	Recorder	9
Constable	41	Register of Bankruptcy	1
Coroner	33	Register of Deeds	2
County Attorney	1	Register of Mesne Conveyances	1
County Clerk	2	Registrar	116
County Commissioner	113	Sheriff	41
County Superintendent of Schools	14	Solicitor	1
County Treasurer	17	Street Commissioner	5
Deputy Sheriff	25	Streetcar Commissioner	1
Detective	2	Tax Collector	35
District Attorney	1	Trustee	2
District Clerk	1	Warden	4
Election Official	52	Weigher	4

TABLE 7: Antebellum Status of Black Officeholders during Reconstruction

STATE	SLAVE	FREE	BOTH	UNKNOWN
Alabama	42	9	8	114
Arkansas	12	5	3	26
Florida	15	8	2	32
District of Columbia	0	6	2	3
Georgia	20	15	5	95
Louisiana	33	81	2	93
Mississippi	59	28	6	131
Missouri	0	0	1	0
North Carolina	22	34	3	126
South Carolina	131	88	5	91
Tennessee	4	7	2	7
Texas	28	6	4	11
Virginia	21	40	12	12
TOTAL	**387**	**327**	**55**	**741**

THE FIRST SOUTH CAROLINA LEGISLATURE AFTER THE 1867 RECONSTRUCTION ACTS

In 1868, South Carolina had the first state legislature with a Black majority. This image includes 63 of the legislature's members, and it was distributed throughout South Carolina by opponents of Radical Reconstruction.[1]

Library of Congress

[1] Julie I. Mellby, "Radical Members of the South Carolina legislature," *Graphic Arts* (blog), entry posted May 19, 2011, http://blogs.princeton.edu/graphicarts/2011/05/radical_members_of_the_south_c.html (accessed October 9, 2014).

"THE HONOURED REPRESENTATIVE OF FOUR MILLIONS OF COLORED PEOPLE"

Please note that this reading contains dehumanizing language. We have chosen to include it in order to honestly communicate the harmful language of the time; however, dehumanizing language should not be spoken or read aloud during class.

Historian Douglas R. Egerton describes the life and political career of Mississippi politician Blanche K. Bruce, the first African American to serve a full six-year term in the United States Senate.

Just ten years after President Abraham Lincoln, in his final public address, advocated voting rights for the "very intelligent [blacks], and on those who serve in our cause as soldiers," Blanche Kelso Bruce, a former slave, raised his right hand to take the oath of office as a U.S. senator from Mississippi. Garbed in a black suit and starched white cotton shirt, his black waistcoat adorned with a fourteen-karat-gold pocket watch, the stout, slightly balding statesman looked older than his thirty-four years. His dark "wavy" hair and newly trimmed van dyke revealed his mother's heritage, while his light skin was the legacy of his father and former master. Preceded in the Senate by Hiram Revels, who had served a partial term from 1870 to 1871, Bruce took his oath less than two decades after Chief Justice Roger B. Taney announced that blacks were not citizens

Portrait of Blanche K. Bruce
Wikimedia Commons

in the country of their birth. "Unpretending and unostentatious," the *Memphis Planet* [newspaper] conceded, "he moves quietly on, the honoured representative of four millions of colored people."

Born in 1841 in Farmville, Virginia, the child then known as Branch and his five siblings were slaves because their mother, Polly Bruce, was a slave. Blanche later insisted that his father, Pettis Perkinson, had treated him as "tenderly" as he had treated his white children, and the young slave—who changed his name to Blanche while still in his teens—was employed as a domestic to his half brother and taught to read. But in an act that demonstrated that the war truly could be a conflict of brothers, in 1861 Blanche's white half brother William left to join the Confederate cause. Blanche decided "to emancipate [him]self" and decamped for the abolitionist stronghold of Lawrence, Kansas, where he found employment as a teacher. The decision nearly proved a fatal one when in August 1863 the town was sacked by Confederate guerrillas led by William Clarke Quantrill. The raiders murdered 183 men and boys, slaughtering anybody above the age of fourteen, but Bruce was able to hide in bushes behind his house. "Quantrill's band certainly would not have spared a colored man," Bruce later wrote.

After the war, Bruce briefly attended Oberlin College, the rural Ohio school widely known for its abolitionist origins and progressive attitudes on educational integration. His meager financial resources soon forced him to withdraw, but while working on a Mississippi River steamboat, Bruce heard about opportunities for ambitious black men in the lower South. Arriving in Mississippi in February 1869, at a time when the state had not yet been readmitted to Congress, Bruce settled in Bolivar County, a devoutly Republican region with a four-to-one advantage in black voters. . . . He quickly won elections for sheriff, then tax collector and superintendent of education, all while editing a local newspaper. Senators were then chosen by state assemblies, and on February 3, 1874, Bruce was chosen by the Mississippi legislature to serve in the national Senate. He journeyed north toward Washington to begin what would become the first full term served by an African American senator. There he joined black Congressmen John Adams Hyman of North Carolina and Robert Smalls, who succeeded Richard "Daddy" Cain in South Carolina's fifth district. Congressman John Roy Lynch, one of the youngest members of the House, continued to represent Mississippi's sixth district. "A turn in fortune's wheel" was one white editor's characterization of just how dramatically the political world had been turned upside down.

As the only man of color in the [Senate] chamber, Bruce sought to position himself as the servant of his state's entire population and dispel any notions that he was a single-issue politician. That meant seeking to appease his state's other senator, James l. Alcorn. Just one month into his term, Bruce stepped across the aisle to converse with Alcorn, a conservative Republican and former Confederate officer who routinely caucused with the chamber's Democrats. Alcorn had not seen fit to honor the tradition of escorting his junior colleague to his swearing-in ceremony, but Bruce was not a man to carry a grudge. The two were engaged in "harmonious conservation" when above them in the gallery, two white observers began to loudly discuss the novelty of "a nigger coming over to sit with Democrats in the United States Senate." The second man, a Marylander, admitted that Bruce "looks clean, and maybe he will keep his place and be respectful." But most senators, well aware of just how far their country had progressed since 1861, accepted his presence, if perhaps grudgingly. "He has made a most favorable impression upon the members of the Senate and those with whom he came into contact," observed one black editor. In politics, power and influence could trump race. If Mississippi Unionists preferred their senator to be white, the reality was that Bruce held the seat, and he shared their vision of regional prosperity, even if they did not share his of an interracial democracy. One Pennsylvania Republican visited Bruce's office and was surprised to find a "small army of white Mississippians" in his waiting room, all of them "ready to swear by you." The northern man thought that curious. He had never before met white southerners, and he "had a lurking idea that these people were all down on a negro on general principles." But Reconstruction was an era of new opportunities, and southern whites, whether they dreaded it or accepted it, had seen this day coming for nearly a decade.[2]

[1] Douglas R. Egerton, *The Wars of Reconstruction: The Brief, Violent History of America's Most Progressive Era* (New York: Bloomsbury Press, 2014), 245–47.

HANDOUT | DOCUMENT
THE ROLE OF "CARPETBAGGERS"

Alexander White, a white congressman from Alabama, described the role that "carpetbaggers" and "scalawags" played in Reconstruction politics as follows:

These white republicans are known by the contemptuous appellation of carpet-bagger and scalawag . . . [T]hey are a northern growth, and unless going South expatriates them, they are still northern men . . . But who are they? . . . Most of them have titles, not empty titles complaisantly bestowed in the piping times of peace, but titles worthily won by faithful and efficient service in the Federal armies, or plucked with strong right arm from war's rugged front upon the field of battle . . . These men either went South with the Union armies and at the close of the war remained there; or went there soon after, in the latter part of 1865 or early in 1866, to make cotton. The high price of cotton in 1865 and 1866, and the facility with which cheap labor could be obtained, induced many enterprising northern men, especially the officers in the Federal armies in the South who had seen and become familiar with the country, to go or remain there to make cotton. Many purchased large plantations and paid large sums of money for them; others rented plantations, in some instances two or three, and embarked with characteristic energy in planting. This, it should be remembered, was before the civil-rights bill or the reconstruction acts, before the colored people had any part in political matters, and two years before they ever proposed to vote or claimed to have the right to vote at any election in the Southern States.

When the political contests of 1868 came on in which the colored people first took part in politics, as near all the native population in the large cotton-growing sections were opposed to negro suffrage and opposed to the republican party, they very naturally turned to these northern men for counsel and assistance in the performance of the new duties and exercise of their newly acquired political rights, and they as naturally gave them such counsel and became their leaders, and were intrusted with official power by them.

This brief summary will give you a correct idea of the manner in which, as I believe, nine-tenths of those who are called carpet-baggers became involved in political affairs [in the] South . . .

Without their co-operation and assistance the colored republicans could neither organize nor operate successfully in political contests, and without them the [Republican] party would soon be extinguished in the Southern States . . .[1]

[1] Excerpted from William E. Gienapp, ed., *The Civil War and Reconstruction: A Documentary Collection* (New York: W. W. Norton, 2001), 374–75.

RECONSTRUCTING MISSISSIPPI

Freedman John Roy Lynch was elected to the Mississippi House of Representatives in the elections of 1868, the first elections in which African Americans voted. In his autobiography, he described the accomplishments of the first interracial legislature in Mississippi.

The [1868] campaign was aggressive from beginning to end . . . [T]he election resulted in a sweeping Republican victory. That party not only elected the state ticket by a majority of about thirty thousand, but also had a large majority in both branches of the state legislature.

The new administration had an important and difficult task before it. A state government had to be organized from top to bottom. A new judiciary had to be inaugurated, consisting of three justices of the state supreme court, fifteen judges of the circuit court, and twenty chancery court judges, all of whom had to be appointed by the governor, by and with the advice and consent of the [state] senate. In addition to this, a new public school system had to be organized and established. There was not a public school building anywhere in the state except in a few of the larger towns, and they, with possibly a few exceptions, were greatly in need of repair. To erect the necessary schoolhouses and to reconstruct and repair those already in existence so as to afford educational facilities for both races was by no means an easy task. It necessitated a very large outlay of cash in the beginning which resulted in a material increase in the rate of taxation for the time being, but the constitution called for the establishment of the system and, of course, the work had to be done. It was not only done, but it was done creditably and as economically as circumstances and conditions at that time made possible. That system, though slightly changed, still stands as a creditable monument to the work of the first Republican state administration that was organized in the state of Mississippi under the Reconstruction Acts of Congress.

It was also necessary to reorganize, reconstruct, and in many instances, rebuild some of the penal, charitable, and other public institutions of the state. A new code of laws also had to be adopted to take the place of the old one, and thus wipe out the black laws that had been passed by what was known as the Johnson legislature. Also it was necessary to change the statutes of the state to harmonize with the new order of things. This was no easy task, especially in view of the fact that a heavy increase in the rate of taxation was thus made necessary. That this great and important work was splendidly, creditably, and economically done, no fair-minded person who is familiar with the facts will question or dispute.[1]

---

[1] From John Hope Franklin, ed., *Reminiscences of an Active Life: The Autobiography of John Roy Lynch* (University Press of Mississippi, 2008), 69–71.

IMPROVING EDUCATION IN SOUTH CAROLINA

Freedman Samuel J. Lee was elected to the South Carolina House of Representatives in the elections of 1868, the first elections in which African Americans voted. He became Speaker of the House in 1872. In 1874, he reported on the improvements to the state education system made by the Republican legislature during Reconstruction.

Permit me, now to refer to our increased educational advantages. It is very pleasing, gentlemen, to witness how rapidly the schools are springing up in every portion of our State, and how the number of competent, well trained teachers are increasing. . . .

Our State University has been renovated and made progressive. New Professors, men of unquestionable ability and erudition, now filled the chairs once filled by men who were too aristocratic to instruct colored youths. A system of scholarships has been established that will, as soon as it is practically in operation, bring into the University a very large number of students. . . . The State Normal School is also situated here, and will have a fair attendance of scholars. We have, also, Claflin University, at Orangeburg, which is well attended, and progressing very favorably; and in the different cities and large towns of the State, school houses have been built, and the school master can be found there busily instructing "the young idea how to shoot" [a quotation from poet James Thomson, who uses *shoot* to mean "grow" or "advance"]. The effects of education can also be perceived; the people are becoming daily more enlightened; their minds are expanding, and they have awakened, in a great degree, from the mental darkness that hitherto surrounded them.[1]

---

[1] Excerpt from Final Report to the South Carolina House, 1874, *Journal of the House of Representatives of the State of South Carolina, for the Regular Session of 1874–1874* (Columbia, 1874), 549–53. Reprinted in William Loren Katz, *Eyewitness* (New York: Simon & Schuster, 1995).

SPEECH BY SUSAN B. ANTHONY: IS IT A CRIME FOR WOMEN TO VOTE?

Susan B. Anthony voted in the 1872 presidential election. Because women did not have the right to vote, she was arrested, put on trial, convicted, and fined $100. The following is an excerpt from a speech she delivered in 1873, prior to her trial.

> *Friends and Fellow-citizens*: I stand before you to-night under indictment for the alleged crime of having voted at the last Presidential election, without having a lawful right to vote. It shall be my work this evening to prove to you that in thus voting, I not only committed no crime, but, instead, simply exercised my *citizen's right*, guaranteed to me and all United States citizens by the national Constitution, beyond the power of any State to deny . . .
>
> The preamble of the federal constitution says: "We, the people of the United States, in order to form a more perfect union, establish justice, insure *domestic* tranquility, provide for the common defense, promote the general welfare and secure the blessings of liberty to ourselves and our posterity, do ordain and establish this constitution for the United States of America."
>
> It was we, the people; not we, the white male citizens; nor yet we, the male citizens; but we, the whole people, who formed this Union. And we formed it, not to give the blessings of liberty, but to secure them; not to the half of ourselves and the half of our posterity, but to the whole people—women as well as men. And it is downright mockery to talk to women of their enjoyment of the blessings of liberty while they are denied the use of the only means of securing them provided by this democratic-republican government—the ballot . . .
>
> To [women], this government has no just powers derived from the consent of the governed. To them this government is not a democracy. It is not a republic. It is an odious aristocracy; a hateful oligarchy of sex. The most hateful aristocracy ever established on the face of the globe. An oligarchy of wealth, where the rich govern the poor; an oligarchy of learning, where the educated govern the ignorant; or even an oligarchy of race, where the Saxon rules the African, might be endured; but this oligarchy of sex, which makes father, brothers, husband, sons, the oligarchs over the mother and sisters, the wife and daughters of every household; which ordains all men sovereigns, all women subjects, carries dissension, discord, and rebellion into every home of the nation . . .

The only question left to be settled, now, is: Are women persons? And I hardly believe any of our opponents will have the hardihood to say they are not. Being persons, then, women are citizens, and no state has a right to make any law, or to enforce any old law, that shall abridge their privileges or immunities. Hence, every discrimination against women in the constitutions and laws of the several states, is to-day null and void, precisely as is every one against negroes . . .[1]

[1] Excerpts from "Is It a Crime for a Citizen of the United States to Vote?" (speech), delivered April 3, 1873, transcribed in Susan Brownell Anthony, *An Account of the Proceedings on the Trial of Susan B. Anthony, on the Charge of Illegal Voting* (Daily Democrat and Chronicle Book Print, 1874), 151–78. Full text available at http://law2.umkc.edu/faculty/projects/ftrials/anthony/anthonyaddress.html.

PLATFORM OF THE WORKINGMEN'S PARTY OF CALIFORNIA (1877)

Please note that this reading contains dehumanizing language. We have chosen to include it in order to honestly communicate the harmful language of the time; however, dehumanizing language should not be spoken or read aloud during class.

The object of this Association is to unite all poor and working men and their friends into one political party, for the purpose of defending themselves against the dangerous encroachments of capital on the happiness of our people and the liberties of our country.

• We propose to wrest the government from the hands of the rich and place it in those of the people, where it properly belongs.

• We propose to rid the country of cheap Chinese labor as soon as possible, and by all the means in our power, because it tends still more to degrade labor and aggrandize capital.

• We propose to destroy land monopoly in our state by such laws as will make it impossible.

• We propose to destroy the great money power of the rich by a system of taxation that will make great wealth impossible in the future.

• We propose to provide decently for the poor and unfortunate, the weak, the helpless, and especially the young, because the country is rich enough to do so, and religion, humanity, and patriotism demand that we should do so.

• We propose to elect none but competent workingmen and their friends to any office whatever. The rich have ruled us until they have ruined us. We will now take our own affairs in our own hands. The republic must and shall be preserved, and only workingmen will do it. Our shoddy aristocrats want an emperor and a standing army to shoot down the people.

• For these purposes, we propose to organize ourselves into the Workingmen's Party of California, and to pledge and enroll therein all who are willing to join us in accomplishing these ends.

• When we have 10,000 members, we shall have the sympathy and support of 20,000 other workingmen.

• The party will then wait upon all who employ Chinese and ask for their discharge, and it will mark as public enemies those who refuse to comply with their request.

• This party will exhaust all peaceable means of attaining its ends, but it will not be denied justice when it has the power to enforce it. It will encourage no riot or outrage, but it will not volunteer to repress, or put down, or arrest, or prosecute the hungry and impatient who manifest their hatred of the Chinamen by a crusade against "John" or those who employ him. let those who raise the storm by their selfishness, suppress it themselves. If they dare raise the devil, let them meet him face to face. We will not help them . . .[1]

[1] Quoted in Ira Brown Cross, *A History of the Labor Movement in California*, vol. 14 (University of California Press, 1935), 96–97. Text available at http://instruct.westvalley.edu/kelly/History20_on_campus/Online%20Readings/Cross_Kearney.htm.

CHINESE IMMIGRANTS WRITE TO PRESIDENT GRANT

Please note that this reading contains dehumanizing language. We have chosen to include it in order to honestly communicate the harmful language of the time; however, dehumanizing language should not be spoken or read aloud during class.

A MEMORIAL FROM REPRESENTATIVE CHINAMEN IN AMERICA TO HIS EXCELLENCY U. S. GRANT, President of the United States of America.

Sir: — In the absence of any consular representative, we, the undersigned, in the name and in behalf of the Chinese people now in America, would most respectfully present for your consideration the following statements regarding the subject of Chinese immigration to this country:

First — We understand that it has always been the settled policy of your honorable government to welcome immigration to your shores, from all countries, without let or hinderance. The Chinese are not the only people who have crossed the ocean to seek a residence in this land.

Second — The treaty of amity and peace between the United States and China makes special mention of the rights and privileges of Americans in China, and also of the rights and privileges of Chinese in America.

Third — American steamers, subsidized by your honorable government, have visited the ports of China, and invited our people to come to this country to find employment and improve their condition.

Fourth — Our people in this country, for the most part, have been peaceable, law-abiding and industrious. They performed the largest part of the unskilled labor in the construction of the Central Pacific Railroad, and also of other railroads on this coast. They have found useful employment in all the manufacturing establishments of this coast, in agricultural pursuits, and in family service. While benefiting themselves with the honest reward of their daily toil, they have given satisfaction to their employers, and have left all the results of their industry to enrich the State. They have not displaced white laborers from these positions, but have simply multiplied industries.

Fifth — The Chinese have neither attempted nor desired to interfere with the established order of things in this country, either of politics or religion. They have opened no whiskey saloons for the purpose of dealing out poison, and degrading their fellow men. They have promptly paid their duties, their taxes, their rents and their debts.

Sixth — It has often occurred, about the time of the State and general elections, that political agitators have stirred up the mind of the people in hostility to the Chinese; but formerly the hostility has subsided after the elections were over.

Seventh — At the present time an intense excitement and bitter hostility against the Chinese in this land, and against further Chinese immigration, has been created in the minds of the people, led on by his Honor the Mayor of San Francisco and his associates in office, and approved by his excellency the Governor of the State and other great men of the State. These great men gathered some twenty thousand of the people of this city together on the evening of April 5, and adopted an address and resolutions against Chinese immigration . . .

Eighth — In this address, numerous charges are made against our people, some of which are highly colored and sensational, and others, having no foundation in fact, are only calculated to mislead honest minds, and create an unjust prejudice against us. We wish most respectfully to call your attention, and through you the attention of Congress, to some of the statements of that remarkable paper, and ask a careful comparison of the statements there made with the facts in the case . . .

> With sentiments of profound respect, LEE MING How, President, Sam yeep Company. LEE CHEE KWAN, President, Yung Wo Company. LAW YEE CHUNG, President, Kong Chow Company. CHAN LEUNG Kox, President, Wing Lung Company. LEE CHEONG CHIP, President, Hop Wu Company. CHANG KONG CHEW, President, Yan Wo Company. LEE TONG HAY, President, Chinese Y. M. C. A.[1]

[1] Excerpted from the "California As I Saw It: First-Person Narratives of California's Early Years, 1849–1900" collection, Library of Congress website. Text available at http://www.loc.gov/teachers/classroommaterials/presentationsandactivities/presentations/timeline/riseind/chinimms/briggs.html (accessed March 22, 2013).

THEY FENCE THEIR NEIGHBORS AWAY

The following is an excerpt from Sioux chief Sitting Bull's speech at the Powder River Council in 1877.

> Behold, my brothers, the spring has come; the earth has received the embraces of the sun and we shall soon see the results of that love! Every seed has awakened and so has all animal life. It is through this mysterious power that we too have our being and we therefore yield to our neighbors, even our animal neighbors, the same right as ourselves, to inhabit this land. Yet hear me, my people, we have now to deal with another race—small and feeble when our fathers first met them, but now great and overbearing. Strangely enough they have a mind to till the soil and the love of possessions is a disease with them . . . They claim this mother of ours, the earth, for their own, and fence their neighbors away; they deface her with their buildings and their refuse. They threaten to take [the land] away from us. My brothers, shall we submit, or shall we say to them: "First kill me before you take possession of my Fatherland."[1]

---

[1] Text available from the Gilder Lehrman Institute of American History, https://www.gilderlehrman.org/sites/default/files/inline-pdfs/Speech%20Excerpts.pdf.

KLANSMEN BROKE MY DOOR OPEN

The following is excerpted from the 1872 testimony of Abram Colby, an African American legislator from Georgia, given before a congressional committee formed to investigate violence against freedpeople in the South.

Colby: On the 29th of October 1869, [the Klansmen] broke my door open, took me out of bed, took me to the woods and whipped me three hours or more and left me for dead. They said to me, "Do you think you will ever vote another damned Radical ticket?" I said, "If there was an election tomorrow, I would vote the Radical ticket." They set in and whipped me a thousand licks more, with sticks and straps that had buckles on the ends of them.

Question: What is the character of those men who were engaged in whipping you?

Colby: Some are first-class men in our town. One is a lawyer, one a doctor, and some are farmers. They had their pistols and they took me in my night-clothes and carried me from home. They hit me five thousand blows. I told President Grant the same that I tell you now. They told me to take off my shirt. I said, "I never do that for any man." My drawers fell down about my feet and they took hold of them and tripped me up. Then they pulled my shirt up over my head. They said I had voted for Grant and had carried the negroes against them. About two days before they whipped me they offered me $5,000 to go with them and said they would pay me $2,500 in cash if I would let another man go to the legislature in my place. I told them that I would not do it if they would give me all the county was worth.

The worst thing was my mother, wife and daughter were in the room when they came. My little daughter begged them not to carry me away. They drew up a gun and actually frightened her to death. She never got over it until she died. That was the part that grieves me the most.

Question: How long before you recovered from the effects of this treatment?

Colby: I have never got over it yet. They broke something inside of me. I cannot do any work now, though I always made my living before in the barber-shop, hauling wood, etc.

Question: You spoke about being elected to the next legislature?

Colby: Yes, sir, but they run me off during the election. They swore they would kill me if I stayed. The Saturday night before the election I went to church. When I got home they just peppered the house with shot and bullets.[1]

---

[1] In Dorothy Sterling, ed., *The Trouble They Seen: The Story of Reconstruction in the Words of African Americans* (Da Capo Press, 1994), 374–75.

ESSENTIAL QUOTE WORKSHEET

1) Your essential quote:	**2) Why did you pick this quote?**
3) What does this quotation reveal about the factors that make violence possible and acceptable in a society?	**4) Your partner's essential quote (describe what is it about):**
5) Link your essential quote to your partner's essential quote. (Does it corroborate, complement, or contradict?)	**6) What does this quotation reveal about the factors that make violence possible and acceptable in a society?**

7) Link your essential quote to someone else's in class. (Does it corroborate, complement, or contradict?)	8) **Final link:** Link your essential quote to one from the handout "The Range of Human Behavior." (Does it corroborate, complement, or contradict?)

A NUCLEUS OF ORDINARY MEN

In his 1935 book *Black Reconstruction in America*, W. E. B. Du Bois analyzes the sources of the power of the Ku Klux Klan this way:

> The method of force which hides itself in secrecy is a method as old as humanity. The kind of thing that men are afraid or ashamed to do openly, and by day, they accomplish secretly, masked, and at night. The method has certain advantages. It uses Fear to cast out Fear; it dares things at which open method hesitates; it may with a certain impunity attack the high and the low; it need hesitate at no outrage of maiming or murder; it shields itself in the mob mind and then throws over all a veil of darkness which becomes glamor. It attracts people who otherwise could not be reached. It harnesses the mob.

> . . . [T]otal depravity, human hate . . . do not explain fully the mob spirit in America. Before the wide eyes of the mob is ever the Shape of Fear. Back of the writhing, yelling, cruel-eyed demons who break, destroy, maim and lynch and burn at the stake, is a knot, large or small, of normal human beings, and these human beings at heart are desperately afraid of something. Of what? Of many things, but usually of losing their jobs, being declassed, degraded, or actually disgraced; of losing their hopes, their savings, their plans for their children; of the actual pangs of hunger, of dirt, of crime. And of all this, most ubiquitous in modern industrial society is that fear of unemployment.

> It is its nucleus of ordinary men that continually gives the mob its initial and awful impetus. Around this nucleus, to be sure, gather snowball-wise all manner of flotsam, filth and human garbage, and every lewdness of alcohol and current fashion. But all this is the horrible covering of this inner nucleus of Fear.[1]

---

[1] W. E. B. Du Bois, *Black Reconstruction in America, 1860–1880* (Free Press, 1999), 677.

COLLABORATORS AND BYSTANDERS

Historian Eric Foner writes that the Ku Klux Klan drew support from many more people than those who directly committed violent or threatening acts against freedpeople and white Republicans. He explains:

> Of course most white southerners did not commit criminal acts, and some spoke out against the Klan. But the large majority of southern whites remained silent. Indeed, the Democratic Party's constant vilification of carpetbaggers and scalawags as corrupt incompetents, their insistence that blacks were unfit for equal citizenship, and their public laments about the intractability of black labor created an atmosphere that made violence seem a legitimate response in the eyes of many white southerners. Community support for the Klan extended to lawyers who represented the criminals in court, editors who established funds for their defense, and the innumerable women who sewed costumes and disguises for them. While most white southerners were law-abiding citizens, they seemed willing to forgive the Klan's excesses because they shared the organization's ultimate goal—the overthrow of Reconstruction and the restoration of white supremacy.[1]

---

[1] Eric Foner, *Forever Free: The Story of Emancipation and Reconstruction* (Vintage Books, 2006), 174.

PROTECTING DEMOCRACY

During the 1871 congressional debate over the Ku Klux Klan Act, Rep. Robert Elliott of South Carolina argued as follows in favor of passing the bill that would allow the federal government to prosecute individuals for acts of political violence and intimidation:

> "The United States shall guaranty to every State in this Union a republican form of government" [a quotation from the constitution].

> To make this clear, let us consider what is "a republican form of government" within the meaning of the constitution? . . . It is a government having a written constitution, or organic law, which provides that its executive and legislative functions shall be exercised by persons elected by the majority of its citizens. In other words, it is a government for the people and by the people.

> Assuming this definition to be correct in substance, I ask, how can a republican government be maintained in a State if the majority of electors are prevented from exercising the elective franchise by force of arms, or if members of the majority, having thus exercised it according to their consciences, are, for that cause, put in terror and subjected to murder, exile, and the lash, through "domestic violence," organized and operated by the minority for the sole purpose of acquiring a political domination in the State? . . .

> . . . If you cannot now protect the loyal men of the South, then have the loyal people of this great Republic done and suffered much in vain, and your free constitution is a mockery and a snare.[1]

---

[1] *Congressional Globe*, House, 42nd cong., 1st sess. (April 1, 1871), 389–92.

HANDOUT | DOCUMENT

RESPONDING TO VIOLENCE: PUBLIC OPINION AND THE LAW

On May 18, 1871, the *Yorkville Enquirer* of South Carolina published the following editorial describing a meeting between Major Lewis Merrill of the US Army and community leaders. Lewis was stationed near Yorkville to monitor Klan violence and gather evidence for possible prosecutions once the Ku Klux Klan Act was passed. After the meeting, the community leaders, many of them members of the Klan themselves, published a call in the *Enquirer* for an end to the violence, but it did not stop. The federal government responded by prosecuting Klan leaders, using Merrill's stockpile of evidence. These prosecutions led to an end of Klan activity for several decades and decreased violence toward supporters of Radical Reconstruction for a few years.

> A number of our citizens, by invitation, visited Major Merrill, post commandant at this place, on Saturday last, to confer upon the subject of the disorderly and turbulent spirit which has prevailed in this section of the State.
>
> Major Merrill expressed his regrets that bands of disguised men had recently been whipping and otherwise maltreating white and colored citizens of this section. He mentioned incidents connected with each of the most recent acts of violence, which impressed those present with the idea that he is kept informed as to the operations of disguised persons in this county. He stated that he had in his possession the names of a number of the parties who had engaged in these lawless acts; and was also in possession of proof amply sufficient to convict some of the persons before any impartial jury. He seemed to be amused at the idea that the names of the guilty parties were not known to the people, and asserted that he could furnish them, and could also have such persons arrested in a few hours. He expressed the belief that the reason why these parties persisted in such acts was the certainty they felt that no person would dare to testify against them; and, in this connection, he exonerated the civil officers at what would appear to be dereliction in the discharge of their duties, by not arresting and bringing to trial the guilty persons. For the reason that victims are afraid to make complaints, no warrants are issued, and consequently the sheriff or other proper officer is powerless to make arrests.
>
> Major Merrill frankly stated that his sole object in asking a conference was that he might induce the influential citizens of the county to adopt prompt and decisive measures to suppress any further disturbance, and thereby avoid the consequences of military interference; that he much preferred that the civil authorities should regulate their own affairs; and that he was satisfied that if the people opposed to lawlessness would unite and sustain each other and the civil authorities in suppressing such acts,

domestic disorder would cease at once. He referred to the fact that a large number of the laborers in the northeastern section of the county were afraid to sleep in their houses, and that such a state of affairs could not longer be tolerated; that he was daily expecting notice that the writ of *habeas corpus* had been suspended in this county, but still hoped, by the timely action of the people, the necessity of declaring martial law would be avoided.

It is now left with our people to say whether or not they intend to regulate their own civil affairs. To succeed in restoring quiet and order, men must no longer withhold their expressed and unequivocal disapprobation. Can we longer permit the best interests of society to be imperiled without a protest, when the remedy is so plain and obvious? All unlawful acts are wrong in principle, and the only difference can be as to the remedy. In this case that remedy lies in public opinion. Let public opinion condemn violent acts as wrong, and society will no longer be afflicted with domestic disorder.

Any further repetition of acts of violence in this county, we feel assured, will be regarded by the military authorities, under the Ku-Klux act, as a denial of the equal protection of law to all of our citizens. The military will proceed, by arresting the supposed guilty parties, to suppress acts of violence, as directed under the Ku-Klux act; and parties, when arrested, will be delivered over to the United States marshal, to be tried before the United States court at Columbia, Charleston or Greenville. Under such circumstances it will be next to impossible to procure bail. The innocent as well as the guilty are liable to be suspected, and the expense of trial in the United States court will necessitate costs in procuring witnesses, counsel fees, &c., that few of our citizens can meet.

The Ku-Klux act comprehends all persons found in disguise, or in unlawful assemblies on the highways, or on the premises of another. The act will be enforced, and rigidly enforced; and unless our people at once determine that there must be no further acts of violence in the county, we will soon have occasion to observe the practical operation of the law in its utmost severity and with all its unpleasant consequences.[1]

---

[1] *Report of and Testimony*, vol. 5, Congress Joint Select Committee on the Condition of Affairs in the Late Insurrectionary States (1872), 1498.

THE RANGE OF HUMAN BEHAVIOR

The quotations below can help us understand the motivations of perpetrators and bystanders in episodes of group violence during Reconstruction.

Psychologist Philip Zimbardo describes the effects of dehumanization:
"Dehumanization occurs whenever some human beings consider other human beings to be excluded from the moral order of being a human person. . . . Under such conditions, it becomes possible for normal, morally upright, and even usually idealistic people to perform acts of destructive cruelty. Not responding to the human qualities of other persons automatically facilitates inhumane actions."

Psychologist Philip Zimbardo describes the effects of anonymity:
"Anything, or any situation, that makes people feel anonymous, as though no one knows who they are or cares to know, reduces their sense of personal accountability, thereby creating the potential for evil action. This becomes especially true when a second factor is added: if the situation or some agency gives them *permission* to engage in antisocial or violent action against others."

Psychologist Ervin Staub discusses the role that shame and humiliation play in violence:
"Individuals, groups, or nations that pride themselves on their power and superiority react strongly when events disconfirm their beliefs about themselves or their image in others' eyes. Shame and humiliation give rise to the motivation to reassert identity and dignity, often by violent means."

Psychologist Ervin Staub discusses the role of bystanders in group violence:
"Bystanders, people who witness but are not directly affected by the actions of perpetrators, help shape society by their reactions. . . . Bystanders can exert powerful influences. They can define the meaning of events and move others toward empathy or indifference. They can promote values and norms of caring, or by their passivity of participation in the system, they can affirm the perpetrators."

[1] Philip Zimbardo, *The Lucifer Effect: Understanding How Good People Turn Evil* (New York: Random House, 2007), 307.

[2] Zimbardo, *The Lucifer Effect*, 301.

[3] Ervin Staub, *Overcoming Evil: Genocide, Violent Conflict, and Terrorism* (Oxford University Press, 2013), 113.

[4] Ervin Staub, *The Roots of Evil: The Origins of Genocide and Other Group Violence* (Cambridge University Press, 1989), 86–87.

DOUGLASS ON MEDIA IMAGES OF AFRICAN AMERICANS

Frederick Douglass wrote the following in 1849, published in his abolitionist newspaper *North Star*:

> Negroes can never have impartial portraits, at the hands of white artists. It seems next to impossible for white men to take likenesses of black men without most grossly exaggerating their distinctive features. Artists, like all other white persons, have adopted a theory respecting the distinctive features of negro physiognomy. We have heard many white persons say that "negroes look all alike," and that they could not distinguish between the old and the young. They associate with the negro face, high cheek bones, distended nostril, depressed nose, thick lips, and retreating foreheads. This theory impressed strongly upon the mind of an artist exercises a powerful influence over his pencil, and very naturally leads him to distort and exaggerate those peculiarities, even when they scarcely exist in the original.[1]

---

[1] Quoted in Joshua Brown, "True Likenesses," in Eric Foner, *Forever Free: The Story of Emancipation and Reconstruction* (Vintage Books, 2006), 35.

"EMANCIPATION" (1865)

Please note that this handout contains dehumanizing imagery. We have chosen to include it in order to honestly communicate the images that the public saw at the time.

Wood engraving by Thomas Nast (1865)

Library of Congress

"FRANCHISE" (1865)

A previous Thomas Nast image entitled "Amnesty" depicts Columbia (the woman who represents the nation) with a group of former Confederates. She asks, "Shall I trust these men?" In the caption to this image, she continues, "And not this man?"

Wood engraving by Thomas Nast (1865)

Library of Congress

"COLORED RULE IN A RECONSTRUCTED(?) STATE" (1874)

Please note that this handout contains dehumanizing imagery. We have chosen to include it in order to honestly communicate the images that the public saw at the time.

How do racial stereotypes in the media create and reinforce "in" groups and "out" groups in a society?

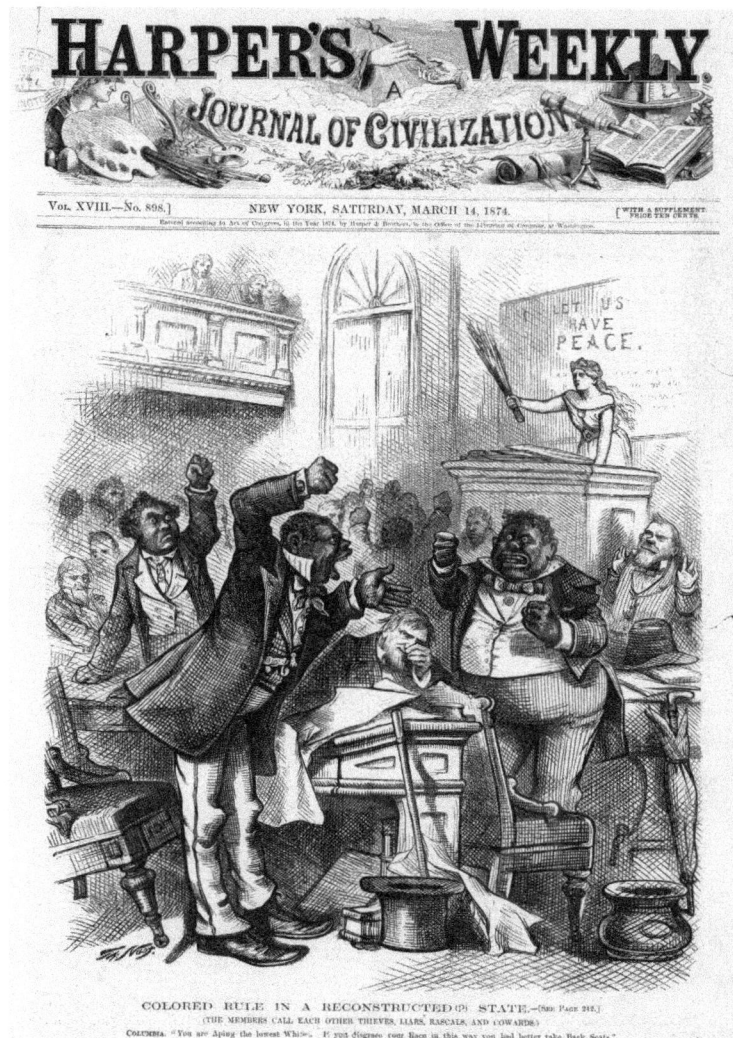

Wood engraving by Thomas Nast (1874)

Library of Congress

"HE WANTS A CHANGE TOO" (1876)

Please note that this handout contains dehumanizing imagery. We have chosen to include it in order to honestly communicate the images that the public saw at the time.

How do racial stereotypes in the media create and reinforce "in" groups and "out" groups in a society?

Wood engraving by Thomas Nast (1876)

The Newberry Digital Collection

SOUTH CAROLINA "RED SHIRTS" BATTLE PLAN (1876)

Democratic Party paramilitary groups also emerged in South Carolina during the 1876 state and national campaigns. There, members of these groups called themselves the "Red Shirts." Their official battle plan, which called for Democratic clubs armed with rifles and pistols, stated in part:

> Every Democrat must feel honor bound to control the vote of at least one negro, by intimidation, purchase, keeping him away.
>
> We must attend every Radical meeting. Democrats must go in as large numbers as they can, and well armed, behave at first with great courtesy and as soon as their speakers begin tell them that they are liars and are only trying to mislead the ignorant negroes.
>
> In speeches to negroes you must remember that they can only be influenced by their fears, superstitions and cupidity. Treat them so as to show them you are the superior race and that their natural position is that of subordination to the white man.
>
> Never threaten a man individually. If he deserves to be threatened, the necessities of the times require that he should die. A dead Radical is very harmless—a threatened Radical is often troublesome, sometimes dangerous, and always vindictive.
>
> Every club must be uniformed in a red shirt and they must be sure and wear it upon all public meetings and particularly on the day of election.[1]

---

[1] In Dorothy Sterling, ed., *The Trouble They Seen: The Story of Reconstruction in the Words of African Americans* (Da Capo Press, 1994), 465.

ELECTION VIOLENCE IN MISSISSIPPI (1875)

Robert Gleeds, an African American candidate for sheriff in Lowndes County, Mississippi, described the violence in his county that occurred on the eve of the 1875 election this way:

> In the latter part of the canvas the young men had a cannon and pistols, very much like an army. The election was wound up on the 2nd of November and on the night before in our city three buildings were set on five and four men killed. Most of the colored people were run out of their houses during the night. It was the worst time we have ever had as far as an election was concerned.
>
> The first fire broke out near my house. I went to work to get my family and as many of my things out as I could. Then a young man came to me and said, "They will kill you when this fire burns low." The next morning a man told me that he did not think it would be safe to go back and I went out in the country and stayed until Saturday after the election. Prior to the election we had a meeting at the courthouse. Dr. Lipscomb and Judge Simms, the candidate on the Democratic side were invited to speak and I had a few words to say myself. I asked, "What could we do? Was there any concession we could make that would secure peace and a quiet election?" Dr. Lipscomb said the way we would have it was by abstaining from voting altogether. Of course I couldn't concede that for others but I was willing to forego any sacrifice as far as I was individually concerned. I told him we used to ask for life and liberty but now if we could just be spared our lives so we could go peacefully along as men and human beings we would be satisfied . . .
>
> It was the most violent time that ever we have seen.[1]

---

[1] In Dorothy Sterling, ed., *The Trouble They Seen: The Story of Reconstruction in the Words of African Americans* (Da Capo Press, 1994), 447–48.

A TEACHER DESCRIBES VIOLENCE AND INTIMIDATION (1875)

Please note that this reading contains dehumanizing language. We have chosen to include it in order to honestly communicate the harmful language of the time; however, dehumanizing language should not be spoken or read aloud during class.

J. L. Edmonds, an African American schoolteacher, gave this account of the murder and intimidation before the 1875 election in Clay County, Mississippi:

> Where we appointed a meeting [the Democrats] would go there and speak as they pleased. They would take a cannon and load it up with chains and leave it with the mouth pointing toward the crowd of colored people. When they fired they had nothing in it more than powder, but when they were going to speak they would have it turned around and chains hanging around it.
>
> They had a parade at West Point. I was standing on the corner talking and some of the colored men came up, and a colored man says, "I do not care how many are riding around, I am a Republican and expect to vote the ticket." Just then a man walked up with a pistol and shot him. Pretty soon another colored man made some expression and he was shot at.
>
> They had flags—red, white, and crimson flags. The whole street was covered. You could not hear your ears hardly for the flags waving and flapping over your head. They had one United States [flag] at the courthouse but most of the flags were just the old confederate flags.
>
> They said they were going to beat at this election. They said that at the meetings, on the stumps and at schoolhouses around the county. They said they would carry the county or kill every nigger. They would carry it if they had to wade in blood.[1]

---

[1] In Dorothy Sterling, ed., *The Trouble They Seen: The Story of Reconstruction in the Words of African Americans* (Da Capo Press, 1994), 450.

ELECTION DAY IN CLINTON MISSISSIPPI (1875)

> *Please note that this reading contains dehumanizing language. We have chosen to include it in order to honestly communicate the harmful language of the time; however, dehumanizing language should not be spoken or read aloud during class.*

State Senator Charles Caldwell was a former slave who had led a company of African American soldiers, earlier in 1875, in a state militia formed to protect freedpeople from the White Line. The militia was later disbanded by the governor as part of a "peace agreement" with the White Line, but attacks and intimidation continued, and Caldwell himself was assassinated later that year. Eugene Welborne, who served as Caldwell's first lieutenant in the militia, gave this account of election day in November 1875 in Clinton, Mississippi, and Caldwell's efforts to ensure a fair vote.

> We could hear in the morning, the cannons commencing to shoot in every direction, just a firing. You could see men with their sixteen-shooters buckled on them charging all through the country. They went in squads.
>
> One crowd would come in from Raymond and say, "One hundred and fifty niggers killed in Raymond; one white man slightly wounded." The guns were firing continually. Word came from Jackson, "The white men have whipped the niggers and run them out."
>
> We did not know what in the world to do. Senator Caldwell was there and I said, "Senator, I think we might just as well give up. We can't do anything here. These men are riding all about the county with their sixteen-shooters." He says, "No. We are going to stay right here. I don't care what they say to you, don't you say a word." We voted as rapidly as we could.
>
> Our votes were pretty strong all day and we would have polled our usual vote, even with all the intimidation, if they would have let us. But our Republicans that were ap-pointed by the board of registration were told that it would not be healthy for them to serve and they made the whole thing Democratic. So when a Republican would come in to vote this fellow looked on the book and said, "I cannot find your name here. Stand aside." They turned off 80 Republicans, one after the other, that way.
>
> I saw Senator Caldwell standing at the door. Said I, "What are you going to do about these registration papers?" "I think," says he, "we will go in and see these fellows." So we went in and spoke to one of the officers. When Mr. Caldwell said, "I know that this man's name was on that book," they said it didn't make any difference what he knew and that he was not going to vote.[1]

---

[1] In Dorothy Sterling, ed., *The Trouble They Seen: The Story of Reconstruction in the Words of African Americans* (Da Capo Press, 1994), 452.

"OF COURSE HE VOTES THE DEMOCRATIC TICKET" (1876)

> *Please note that this handout contains dehumanizing imagery. We have chosen to include it in order to honestly communicate the images that the public saw at the time.*

This image appeared in *Harper's Weekly* in 1876. The caption reads:

"Of course he wants to vote the Democratic ticket!"

Democratic "Reformer": "You're as free as air, ain't you?
Say you are or I'll blow yer black head off!"

Wood engraving by Thomas Nast from *Harper's Weekly* (1876)

The Newberry Digital Collection

"LONG VIEW: NEGRO" BY LANGSTON HUGHES

Emancipation: 1865

Sighted through the

telescope of dreams

Looms larger,

So much larger,

So it seems,

Than truth can be.

But turn the telescope around,

Look through the larger end—

And wonder why

What was so large

Becomes so small

Again[1]

---

[1] In *The Collected Works of Langston Hughes: The Poems, 1951–1967*, vol. 3 (University of Missouri, 2001), 152.

RESTRICTING THE VOTE AND DIVIDING SOCIETY

The Democratic Party's takeover of Southern state legislatures in the 1870s spurred a near total reversal of Reconstruction's hard-won civil rights victories. For almost a generation after the end of Reconstruction, most eligible Black voters in the South had exercised their right to vote, despite the coordinated efforts of white supremacists who used violence and terror to try to deny them that right.

But beginning in the 1890s, state houses throughout the former Confederacy passed a flurry of legislation aimed at restricting the Black vote. In accord with the Fifteenth Amendment, which prohibited granting suffrage on the basis of race, these measures were written to target African Americans without mentioning race as the basis for denying them the vote. Instead they restricted voting based on economics, education, and other factors that legislators knew would include most Black citizens, even if they also excluded some white citizens.

The measures included strict residency requirements and poll taxes, which were out of reach for the vast majority of African Americans still struggling to gain an economic foothold after slavery. Literacy tests—designed to measure a prospective voter's knowledge of the state constitution and always administered by a white election official—were also widespread. Grandfather clauses, which decided a voter's eligibility based on whether his grandfather could vote, blatantly targeted African Americans. All in all, these laws resulted in the nearly total disenfranchisement of Black Americans, and a significant number of white Americans, in the South.

In the 1896 case *Plessy v. Ferguson*, the US Supreme Court ruled against Homer Plessy, an African American man who sought to challenge segregation on streetcars. Eight of the nine Supreme Court justices argued that separate facilities for Black Americans do not violate their rights so long as the facilities are equal to those provided for white Americans.

The *Plessy* decision had far reaching consequences, permitting the growth of a system of state and local laws known as "Jim Crow" laws. Whereas state governments throughout the South had long established racial separation in schools and other institutions, the ruling in *Plessy* represented the first time that the federal government gave its stamp of approval to such laws. In response, state governments went about instituting segregation in almost every aspect of life. In many places, Black and white Americans could not publicly sit, drink, or eat side by side. Churches, theaters, parks, even cemeteries were segregated. "By the early 1900s," writes historian Lerone Bennett, Jr. "America was two nations—one white, one black, separate and unequal."[1]

---

[1] Lerone Bennett, Jr., Before the Mayflower: A History of Black America (New York: Penguin Books, 1984), 256.

W. E. B. DU BOIS REFLECTS ON THE PURPOSE OF HISTORY

The following is an excerpt from a chapter titled "The Propaganda of History" in W. E. B. Du Bois's influential 1935 book *Black Reconstruction in America*.

How the facts of American history have in the last half century been falsified because the nation was ashamed. The South was ashamed because it fought to perpetuate human slavery. The North was ashamed because it had to call in the black men to save the Union, abolish slavery and establish democracy.

What are American children taught today about Reconstruction? . . . [A]n American youth attending college today would learn from current textbooks of history that the Constitution recognized slavery; that the chance of getting rid of slavery by peaceful methods was ruined by the Abolitionists; that after the period of Andrew Jackson, the two sections of the United States "had become fully conscious of their conflicting interests. Two irreconcilable forms of civilization . . . ." He would read that Harriet Beecher Stowe brought on the Civil War; that the assault on Charles Sumner was due to his "coarse invective" against a South Carolina Senator; and that Negroes were the only people to achieve emancipation with no effort on their part. That Reconstruction was a disgraceful attempt to subject white people to ignorant Negro rule . . .

In other words, he would in all probability complete his education without any idea of the part which the black race has played in America; of the tremendous moral problem of abolition; of the cause and meaning of the Civil War and the relation which Reconstruction had to democratic government and the labor movement today . . .

War and especially civil strife leave terrible wounds. It is the duty of humanity to heal them. It was therefore soon conceived as neither wise nor patriotic to speak of all the causes of strife and the terrible results to which national differences in the United States had led. And so, first of all, we minimized the slavery controversy which convulsed the nation from the Missouri Compromise down to the Civil War. On top of that, we passed by Reconstruction with a phrase of regret or disgust.

But are these reasons of courtesy and philanthropy sufficient for denying truth? If history is going to be scientific, if the record of human action is going to be set down with the accuracy and faithfulness of detail which will allow its use as a measuring rod and guidepost for the future of nations, there must be set some standards of ethics in research and interpretation.

If, on the other hand, we are going to use history for our pleasure and amusement, for inflating our national ego, and giving us a false but pleasurable sense of accomplishment, then we must give up the idea of history as a science or as an art using the results of science, and admit frankly that we are using a version of historic fact in order to influence and educate the new generation along the way we wish.

It is propaganda like this that has led men in the past to insist that history is "lies agreed upon"; and to point out the danger in such misinformation. It is indeed extremely doubtful if any permanent benefit comes to the world through such action. Nations reel and stagger on their way; they make hideous mistakes; they commit frightful wrongs; they do great and beautiful things. And shall we not best guide humanity by telling the truth about all this, so far as the truth is ascertainable?[1]

[1] W. E. B. Du Bois, *Black Reconstruction in America, 1860–1880* (Free Press, 1999), 711–14.

WE NEED TO TALK ABOUT AN INJUSTICE

Democracy is shaped by individuals who champion issues they believe are important to them and their society. Alabama lawyer Bryan Stevenson has devoted his life to correcting injustices in the American criminal justice system. In his speech at a 2012 TED conference,[1] Stevenson explained the experiences and beliefs that inspire his work. The following is an excerpt.

I grew up in a house that was the traditional African American home that was dominated by a matriarch, and that matriarch was my grandmother. She was tough, she was strong, she was powerful. She was the end of every argument in our family. She was the beginning of a lot of arguments in our family. She was the daughter of people who were actually enslaved. Her parents were born in slavery in Virginia in the 1840s. She was born in the 1880s and the experience of slavery very much shaped the way she saw the world. . . .

And I remember, when I was about eight or nine years old, waking up one morning, going into the living room, and all of my cousins were running around. And my grandmother was sitting across the room staring at me. And at first I thought we were playing a game. And I would look at her and I'd smile, but she was very serious. And after about 15 or 20 minutes of this, she got up and she came across the room and she took me by the hand and she said, "Come on, Bryan. You and I are going to have a talk." And I remember this just like it happened yesterday. I never will forget it.

She took me out back and she said, "Bryan, I'm going to tell you something, but you don't tell anybody what I tell you." I said, "Okay, Mama." She said, "Now you make sure you don't do that." I said, "Sure." Then she sat me down and she looked at me and she said, "I want you to know I've been watching you." And she said, "I think you're special." She said, "I think you can do anything you want to do." I will never forget it.

And then she said, "I just need you to promise me three things, Bryan." I said, "Okay, Mama." She said, "The first thing I want you to promise me is that you'll always love your mom." She said, "That's my baby girl, and you have to promise me now you'll always take care of her." Well I adored my mom, so I said, "Yes, Mama. I'll do that." Then she said, "The second thing I want you to promise me is that you'll always do the right thing even when the right thing is the hard thing." And I thought about it and I said, "Yes, Mama. I'll do that." Then finally she said, "The third thing I want you to promise me is that you'll never drink alcohol." (Laughter.) Well I was nine years old, so I said, "Yes, Mama. I'll do that."

. . . And I'm going to admit something to you . . . I'm 52 years old, and I'm going to admit to you that I've never had a drop of alcohol. (Applause.) I don't say that because

I think that's virtuous; I say that because there is power in identity. When we create the right kind of identity, we can say things to the world around us that they don't actually believe makes sense. We can get them to do things that they don't think they can do. When I thought about my grandmother, of course she would think all her grandkids were special. My grandfather was in prison during prohibition. My male uncles died of alcohol-related diseases. And these were the things she thought we needed to commit to.

Well I've been trying to say something about our criminal justice system. This country is very different today than it was 40 years ago. In 1972, there were 300,000 people in jails and prisons. Today, there are 2.3 million. The United States now has the highest rate of incarceration in the world. We have seven million people on probation and parole. And mass incarceration, in my judgment, has fundamentally changed our world. In poor communities, in communities of color there is this despair, there is this hopelessness, that is being shaped by these outcomes. One out of three black men between the ages of 18 and 30 is in jail, in prison, on probation or parole. In urban communities across this country—Los Angeles, Philadelphia, Baltimore, Washington—50 to 60 percent of all young men of color are in jail or prison or on probation or parole.

Our system isn't just being shaped in these ways that seem to be distorting around race, they're also distorted by poverty. We have a system of justice in this country that treats you much better if you're rich and guilty than if you're poor and innocent. Wealth, not culpability, shapes outcomes. And yet, we seem to be very comfortable. The politics of fear and anger have made us believe that these are problems that are not our problems. We've been disconnected.

It's interesting to me. We're looking at some very interesting developments in our work. My state of Alabama, like a number of states, actually permanently disenfranchises you if you have a criminal conviction. Right now in Alabama 34 percent of the black male population has permanently lost the right to vote. We're actually projecting in another 10 years the level of disenfranchisement will be as high as it's been since prior to the passage of the Voting Rights Act. And there is this stunning silence . . .

I talk a lot about these issues . . . And it's interesting, when I teach my students about African American history, I tell them about slavery. I tell them about terrorism, the era that began at the end of Reconstruction that went on to World War II. We don't really know very much about it. But for African Americans in this country, that was an era defined by terror. In many communities, people had to worry about being lynched. They had to worry about being bombed. It was the threat of terror that shaped their lives. And these older people come up to me now and they say, "Mr. Stevenson, you give talks, you make speeches, you tell people to stop saying we're dealing with terrorism for the first time in our nation's history after 9/11." They tell me to say, "No, tell them that we grew up with that." And that era of terrorism, of course, was followed by segregation and decades of racial subordination . . .

And yet, we have in this country this dynamic where we really don't like to talk about our problems. We don't like to talk about our history. And because of that, we really haven't understood what it's meant to do the things we've done historically. We're constantly running into each other. We're constantly creating tensions and conflicts. We have a hard time talking about race, and I believe it's because we are unwilling to commit ourselves to a process of truth and reconciliation. In South Africa, people understood that we couldn't overcome apartheid without a commitment to truth and reconciliation . . .

. . . Well I believe that our identity is at risk. That when we actually don't care about these difficult things, the positive and wonderful things are nonetheless implicated. We love innovation. We love technology. We love creativity. We love entertainment. But ultimately, those realities are shadowed by suffering, abuse, degradation, marginalization. And for me, it becomes necessary to integrate the two. Because ultimately we are talking about a need to be more hopeful, more committed, more dedicated to the basic challenges of living in a complex world. And for me that means spending time thinking and talking about the poor, the disadvantaged . . . But thinking about them in a way that is integrated in our own lives.

You know ultimately, we all have to believe things we haven't seen. We do. As rational as we are, as committed to intellect as we are. Innovation, creativity, development comes not from the ideas in our mind alone. They come from the ideas in our mind that are also fueled by some conviction in our heart. And it's that mind-heart connection that I believe compels us to not just be attentive to all the bright and dazzly things, but also the dark and difficult things. Vaclav Havel, the great Czech leader, talked about this. He said, "When we were in eastern Europe and dealing with oppression, we wanted all kinds of things, but mostly what we needed was hope, an orientation of the spirit, a willingness to sometimes be in hopeless places and be a witness . . ."

I had the great privilege, when I was a young lawyer, of meeting Rosa Parks. And Ms. Parks used to come back to Montgomery every now and then, and she would get together with two of her dearest friends, these older women, Johnnie Carr who was the organizer of the Montgomery bus boycott—amazing African American woman— and Virginia Durr, a white woman, whose husband, Clifford Durr, represented Dr. King. And these women would get together and just talk.

And every now and then Ms. Carr would call me, and she'd say, "Bryan, Ms. Parks is coming to town. We're going to get together and talk. Do you want to come over and listen?" And I'd say, "Yes, Ma'am, I do." And she'd say, "Well what are you going to do when you get here?" I said, "I'm going to listen." And I'd go over there and I would, I would just listen. It would be so energizing and so empowering.

And one time I was over there listening to these women talk, and after a couple of hours Ms. Parks turned to me and she said, "Now Bryan, tell me what the Equal Justice Initiative is. Tell me what you're trying to do." And I began giving her my rap. I said, "Well we're trying to challenge injustice. We're trying to help people who have been wrongly convicted. We're trying to confront bias and discrimination in the administration of criminal justice. We're trying to end life without parole sentences for children. We're trying to do something about the death penalty. We're trying to reduce the prison population. We're trying to end mass incarceration."

I gave her my whole rap, and when I finished she looked at me and she said, "Mmm mmm mmm." She said, "That's going to make you tired, tired, tired." (Laughter.) And that's when Ms. Carr leaned forward, she put her finger in my face, she said, "That's why you've got to be brave, brave, brave."

. . . We need to find ways to embrace these challenges, these problems, the suffering. Because ultimately, our humanity depends on everyone's humanity. I've learned very simple things doing the work that I do. It's just taught me very simple things. I've come to understand and to believe that each of us is more than the worst thing we've ever done. I believe that for every person on the planet. I think if somebody tells a lie, they're not just a liar. I think if somebody takes something that doesn't belong to them, they're not just a thief. I think even if you kill someone, you're not just a killer. And because of that there's this basic human dignity that must be respected by law. I also believe that in many parts of this country, and certainly in many parts of this globe, that the opposite of poverty is not wealth. I don't believe that. I actually think, in too many places, the opposite of poverty is justice.

And finally, I believe that, despite the fact that it is so dramatic and so beautiful and so inspiring and so stimulating, we will ultimately not be judged by our technology, we won't be judged by our design, we won't be judged by our intellect and reason. Ultimately, you judge the character of a society, not by how they treat their rich and the powerful and the privileged, but by how they treat the poor, the condemned, the incarcerated. Because it's in that nexus that we actually begin to understand truly profound things about who we are.[2]

---

[1] TED ("Technology, Entertainment, Design") is a nonprofit organization that sponsors conferences comprised of short talks by leaders and thinkers from a variety of disciplines.

[2] Bryan Stevenson, "We Need to Talk About an Injustice," speech presented at TED Conference, March 2012, available at https://www.ted.com/talks/bryan_stevenson_we_need_to_talk_about_an_injustice/transcript (accessed May 28, 2014).

A LIFELINE FOR DEMOCRACY

Ruth Simmons was born into an East Texas family of sharecroppers in the 1940s. In her 2005 commencement speech at the University of Vermont, excerpted below, she describes experiences that helped her escape the poverty and discrimination of her youth to become the president of Brown University.

> In my estimation, there is no greater benefit to a child nor greater boon to any nation than the provision of education to every citizen. Education develops intellectual resources, makes possible the advancement of knowledge helpful to society's wellbeing, and assures the innovation so necessary to ongoing economic vitality. Education prompts the development of capacities that would often otherwise lie fallow, and nurtures a respect for reason and civility, both important to maintaining peace and stability throughout the world. As a personal benefit, education helps one establish a healthy relationship with the broader world. For me, education has done all of this and so much more. Rescuing me from intellectual hunger and deprivation, it has given me the tools to understand the context into which I was born, and positioned me to surpass the limitations imposed on me by history and circumstance. . . .

> In 1951 when I started grade school in rural East Texas, the America that I knew was penuriously exploitative, shockingly bigoted, deeply and hypocritically divided along racial lines, and headed for national disaster. My father and mother were living at the time in a small four-room house atop a knoll overlooking the sprawling, fertile cotton fields where they worked as laborers. Neither of them had been schooled beyond the eighth grade. Eleven children had preceded me in our household, so when I arrived there were naturally expressions of exasperation by the older children who understood the consequences of yet another mouth to feed. I was delivered by Miss Addie Bryant, who, as a midwife, was one of the most respected people in our small community. In a community where no one was well educated, a midwife was considered to be in the upper echelon of society. My older sisters and brothers had only occasional opportunity to attend school; the primary responsibility of everyone in our sharecropping family, including the smallest children, was to harvest cotton so, when there was work to do in the fields, school attendance suffered. As a result, few of us were able to attend school with enough frequency to graduate from high school.

> But I was lucky. I began school at a time when the cotton gin was taking hold, causing sharecroppers to seek opportunities for employment in cities. Before my parents would make the move to Houston, where I received most of my schooling, I was introduced to education at W. R. Banks School for Colored Children. That first year was an introduction to a world that I could scarcely believe existed: a world where brawn had little bearing, where winning was encouraged, and where no limitations marred achievement. Little could I have imagined the path that I would take as a result of Miss Ida Mae initiating me into a new and exciting world of learning.

Miss Ida Mae Henderson was renowned for her teaching. I don't know if the principal deliberately chose her for first graders because of her inviting personality but everyone I have heard speak of her lights up when they recall their time in Miss Ida Mae's class. What struck one most about her persona was her extraordinary enthusiasm for her students. I had never met anyone so enthusiastic about learning and so full of fervor for the achievement of children. Imagine a rag tag group of poor country children, dressed in tatters, wearing shoes held together with string and minimally nourished. Now imagine them, too, sitting in a bright, cheerfully decorated classroom with a teacher whose attitude and voice bespoke joy at the presence of these children. If you can imagine this miracle, you can possibly appreciate why the sunshine from Miss Ida Mae's voice and smile transfixed us, making us want to bask in that kind of radiance, hopefulness and confidence forever. That is how I came to love learning, by watching someone else who had been infused with the spirit of learning.

Miss Ida Mae was the first person I met who was college educated and, although I did not understand at the time why she was so different from anything I had ever known, I knew that education had wrought something wondrous in her. That something was a delight in learning and in imparting that knowledge to others. The luminescence that radiated from her respect and enthusiasm for learning drew us in. Absorbing her every instruction, I worked hard to secure abundant praise from her, and was convinced that something momentous was happening to my life now that she was in it. With her as my tour guide, I thought I had been given keys to a magic kingdom long before I heard of Walt Disney's. In this kingdom, I was free to go anywhere without worrying about racial restrictions. All the limitations my parents had known fell away as I grasped the power of my mind to push aside the barriers they had experienced and had anticipated for me.

Arriving in Houston the next year, I discovered miraculously that Miss Ida Mae was not the only teacher who was dedicated, uplifting, forceful and self-confident. There were many others with high standards, excellent skills and charismatic personalities who were every-day models for life. Mrs. Caraway, Mrs. Washington, Mrs. Parish, Mr. Saunders, Mrs. Lillie and so many more like them filled my years of public school with admonitions concerning hard work and high attainment. These teachers, working in the inner city schools, did the work of social workers, philanthropists, mentors, counselors, advocates, civic icons, and moral exemplars. They formed a tightly knit network of care that kept communities going and, most importantly, kept the promise of social change and civil rights alive. Though their efforts, change did come.

I recall this story every day as a reminder of the power of education. . . . Learning makes possible the most daunting and elusive change. If you have not discovered that yet, you will learn it in myriad ways over the coming years. Because you have enlarged your reach through learning, you will have the opportunity to influence others in the way teachers changed my life. The light that shone from Miss Ida Mae has lit my path for over forty years. What is the light that you will shine for others? By the way you respect yourself and others? By the way you care for your family? By the openness you have to difference? By the gratitude and humility you show for what you have been given? By the winning spirit that you bring to everything you do? . . .

Teachers remain at the heart of any education that takes root on the one hand and uplifts on the other. They do not merely provide tools or point out which path to take on this voyage. They pack our bags, set us on our way, and give us maps for the most scenic ride of our lives. Along the way we see the history of the world unfold. We see the beauty of what god and man have produced. We learn the elements of design and harmony that give greater meaning and enjoyment to our lives.

We see how problems are solved and conflicts are abated. We see the tragic consequences of bigotry, want, and human degradation. Each of us has had a moment of recognition when we understood the value of learning. To have a guide in that process who not only leads us to shore but repeatedly casts us back upon the sea until we can find our own way back to shore is of defining importance. Teaching, wherever it occurs, is a lifeline for individuals, communities, nations, the world.[1]

[1] Ruth J. Simmons, speech presented at the University of Vermont (Burlington, VT), May 29, 2005, available at http://www.uvm.edu/president/ceremonies/commencement2005/?Page=fogel_commencementaddress05.html (accessed October 10, 2014).

EVIDENCE CHART

INITIAL CLAIM

What is your opening claim about the promise of Emancipation and to what extent it was fulfilled by Reconstruction?	

EVIDENCE

What evidence do you have from the sources you investigated to support your initial claim? Make sure to cite your sources.	

DOUBLE CHECK

What ideas from the sources contradict your claims? Have you forgotten anything? Make sure to cite your sources.	

SAMPLE COUNTERARGUMENT WORKSHEET

WORD BANK

Useful language to use when making and refuting counterarguments

Nevertheless	Some might believe	But	Even so	Despite
On the one hand	On the other hand	While	It is true	Yet
In contrast	To some extent	Although	Admittedly	However
It might seem that	What this argument fails to account for			

1. Argument This thesis is true because . . .	
2. Counterargument Yet some people argue . . .	
3. Refutation But . . .	
4. Response On the other hand . . .	

OUTLINING YOUR ESSAY: GRAPHIC ORGANIZER FOR BODY PARAGRAPH

OUTLINE FOR BODY PARAGRAPH #: _____

THESIS (The purpose of my paper is to prove . . .)

ARGUMENT (This thesis is true because . . .)

Evidence to support argument (with citation):	**Analysis:** This evidence supports my argument because . . .
1.	
2.	
3.	

(optional)

COUNTERARGUMENT (Some people argue . . .)

Evidence to support argument (with citation):	Analysis: This evidence supports my argument because . . .
1.	
2.	
3.	

FACING HISTORY & OURSELVES

SHARING OUR LEARNING: WRITING CONNECTIONS

WRITING CONNECTION 1
(DAY 6)

What does it mean to be free?

DIRECTIONS: Create a concept map for *freedom*, highlighting the characteristics that represent aspirations expressed by freedpeople.

WRITING CONNECTION 2
(DAY 8)

What were the objectives of Reconstruction?

DIRECTIONS: Write a paragraph describing the objectives of Reconstruction and explaining the measures you would use to assess Reconstruction's success or failure.

_____

_____

_____

_____

_____

_____

_____

_____

_____

_____

_____

_____

_____

_____

_____

_____

_____

WRITING CONNECTION 3
(DAY 12)

How did Reconstruction advance interracial democracy and equality for African Americans?

DIRECTIONS: Write a paragraph, supported with evidence, explaining how Reconstruction advanced interracial democracy and equality for African Americans.

_____

_____

_____

_____

_____

_____

_____

_____

_____

_____

_____

_____

_____

_____

_____

WRITING CONNECTION 4
(DAY 13)

Can democracy exist without equality?

DIRECTIONS: Hold a class discussion and make an evidence-based claim about whether democracy can exist without equality.

WRITING CONNECTION 5
(DAYS 18 + 19)

What was the greatest challenge confronting the nation in the progress toward freedom and equality for all during Reconstruction?

DIRECTIONS: Develop an evidence-based claim about the greatest challenge to equality during and after Reconstruction, and demonstrate your thinking in a structured discussion.

WRITING CONNECTION 6
(DAY 22)

Why has democracy been called an "eternal struggle"?

DIRECTIONS: Participate in a Socratic seminar about what can be done today to complete the unfinished work of Reconstruction and fulfill the promise of Emancipation.

FINAL WRITING CONNECTION & TAKING INFORMED ACTION

Essential Question: What was the promise of Emancipation? To what extent was it fulfilled by Reconstruction?

WRITING PROMPT

In an essay, construct an argument that addresses the essential question using specific claims and relevant evidence from historical and contemporary sources while acknowledging competing views.

INFORMED ACTION

In a hands-on project, students will apply lessons gained from their study of Reconstruction toward understanding contemporary challenges to freedom and equality. The informed action has three parts:

> **UNDERSTAND:** Pick a topic of debate that was central to the struggle for freedom and equality during Reconstruction and continues to be debated today. Examples of issues that were important during Reconstruction include but are not limited to:
>
> - Education
>
> - Political participation and citizenship (voting and office holding)
>
> - Economic equality
>
> - Equal protection of the law
>
> - The criminal justice system

> **ASSESS:** In a group of three to five students, conduct outside research to learn more about how your chosen topic is being discussed and debated today. What are some of the important positions and perspectives on the topic? Who are key experts and stakeholders? What echoes of the Reconstruction era do you recognize in the debate today (both in the challenges faced and the solutions people are proposing to address the challenges)?

ACT: In the same group, create a plan for organizing a public forum to educate a community (classroom, school, or neighborhood) about your chosen topic. Your group's plan should address the following questions:

- Whom will you invite to speak, and whom will you invite to be in the audience? Be sure to identify the local experts on the topic, who is directly impacted, and who might be capable of effecting change. You may also want to consider whether you'll invite speakers with opposing viewpoints. If not, how will you offer the audience an opportunity to consider multiple perspectives?

- What will be the venue and location for the forum? How will the location help you reach your intended audience?

- What questions will you ask the speakers? How will your questions address the most important aspects of the debate?

- How will you structure the agenda for the forum? How much time will you give for community members to weigh in? How much time for speakers?

www.ingramcontent.com/pod-product-compliance
Lightning Source LLC
Chambersburg PA
CBHW060903090426
42738CB00026B/3500